A
GRAMMAR
ARMENIAN AND ENGLISH

A GRAMMAR ARMENIAN AND ENGLISH

BY

P. PASCHAL AUCHER

D. D.

GYAN

Published by

Gyan Publishing House
5, Ansari Road
Daryaganj, New Delhi-110002
Phone: 011-47034999, 9811692060
E-mail: books@gyanbooks.com

Distribution Network
gyanbooks.com
India, USA, Canada, UK, Australia, France

ISBN: 978-81-212-7949-9 (PB)
First Published, 1819

2nd Impression 2023

Printed at: Gyan Press, Delhi.

A GRAMMAR ARMENIAN AND ENGLISH
Author: P. PASCHAL AUCHER

A
GRAMMAR
ARMENIAN AND ENGLISH

A
GRAMMAR
ARMENIAN AND ENGLISH

BY

P. PASCHAL AUCHER

D. D.

VENICE

printed at the Armenian press

OF ST. LAZARUS

—

1832

ADVERTISEMENT

The Author having published in 1819. the first Edition of his Armenian Grammar for the use of English Students of that language, is encouraged to republish it in a more correct and complete form.

In the present Edition will be found some specimens of Armenian Poetry, and some translations of Lord Byron from the Armenian into English; and there are added, by way of exercise, Extracts from the best Armenian Writers. Some of which are accompanied also with English translations.

It is therefore hoped that the Volume in its present form will prove an acquisition, and meet with a continuance of public approbation.

Եւ նստաւ Տապանն .... ՚ի լերինս Արարատայ ։

Ծննդ. Ը. 4.

And the Ark rested .... upon the mountains of Ararat.

Gen. VIII. 4.

A

GRAMMAR

Grammar teaches the art of speaking and writing correctly.

Human discourse is formed of letters, syllables and words.

Letters are the elements of a syllable.

A syllable is either one letter, or the union of letters.

A word is one or more syllables, which express some thing.

The union of words to explain our thoughts completely is called discourse.

The harmony of words with the rules of Grammar is called Syntax.

ALPHABET.

The Armenian Alphabet consists of thirty-eight letters.

Form.			*Name.*	*Sound.*
Ա	ա	ա	Ipe (as in *ripe*)	A (as in *father.*)
Բ	բ	բ	pien,	P soft.
Գ	գ	գ	kim,	K, C, Q.
Դ	դ	դ	tah,	T soft.
Ե	ե	ե	yetch,	YE (as in *yes.*)
Զ	զ	զ	zah,	Z or S soft.
Է	է	է	é,	E (as in *met.*)
Ը	ը	ը	yet, like French *e* mute, or as english	U (in *us.*)
Թ	թ	թ	twoh,	T hard.
Ժ	ժ	ժ	j (french, or *zh* or as english *s* in the words *pleasure, measure, confusion.*)	
Ի	ի	ի	inui,	I or E.
Լ	լ	լ	liune,	L.
Խ	խ	խ	khé,	CH german, or as χ greek.
Ծ	ծ	ծ	dzah,	DZ.
Կ	կ	կ	ghien,	G hard.
Հ	հ	հ	hwoh,	H.
Ձ	ձ	ձ	tzah,	TZ soft.
Ղ	ղ	ղ	ghahd,	GH or as γ greek.
Ճ	ճ	ճ	jé *or* jdé,	J or G soft.
Մ	մ	մ	mien,	M.
Յ	յ	յ	he *or* ye,	H soft.

Ն	ն	ն	noo,	N.
Շ	շ	շ	shah,	SH.
Ո	ո	ո	wo,	WO (as in *worthy*.)
Չ	չ	չ	tchah,	TCH or CH (as in *fetch* or *charity*.)
Պ	պ	պ	bé,	B.
Ջ	ջ	ջ	tché *or* ché,	CH or TCH soft.
Ռ	ռ	ռ	rah,	R hard (as in *raft*.)
Ս	ս	ս	sé,	S.
Վ	վ	վ	viev,	V.
Տ	տ	տ	dune,	D.
Ր	ր	ր	ré,	R soft.
Ց	ց	ց	tzvoh,	TZ hard.
Ւ	ւ	ւ	une,	U.
Փ	փ	փ	pure,	P.
Ք	ք	ք	ké,	K or CH (as in *archangel* and *chaos*.)
Օ	օ	օ	o,	O.
Ֆ	ֆ	ֆ	pha *or* fé,	PH or F. [1]

The 36 Characters from Ա to Ք were formed in the fourth Century, the last two Օ and Ֆ were introduced into the Armenian Alphabet in the twelfth Century.

Vowels.

ա, ե, է, ը, ի, ո, ւ, օ.

1 The above sounds are the nearest that can be given in English characters.

Consonants.

բ, գ, դ, զ, թ, ժ, լ, խ, ծ, կ, հ, ձ, ղ, ճ, մ, յ, ն, շ, չ, պ, ջ, ռ, ս, վ, տ, ր, ց, փ, ք, ֆ.

SYLLABLE.

A syllable is an articulate sound, as, առ, *ar*. նա, *nah*. դար, *tar*. աղտ, *aghd*. որմ, *worm*. բարդ, *part*. գառն, *karn*. դէմք, *temk*. զօր, *zor*. ընդ, *unt*. թիւ, *tiv*. ժամ, *zham*. լոյս, *looyce*. ծառ, *dzar*. կալ, *gahl*. հայր, *hire*. ձայն, *tzine*. ճառ, *jar*. մայր, *mire*. շուն, *shoon*. չար, *tchar*. ջուր, *tshoor* or *chure*. սուրբ, *soorp*. տէր, *der*. րամ, *rahm*. ցու, *tzoo*. ւիւթ, *ute* or *ewt*. փառք, *park*.

A syllable may be also composed of six letters, as սեամբք, *siampk*. ջուրբք, *chiurpk*.

Two or three consonants are sometimes formed before or after a vowel.

Double consonants at the end of a syllable are pronounced short, as, տարր, *darr*. քաղաքք, *cahghack*.

When the word ends with double ն, in the pronunciation an ը is inserted, as, մատնն (մատնըն) *madnun*. ձեռնն (ձեռնըն) *tziernun*.

So also when in the beginning of a word the same consonant is doubled, as, շշուկ (շըշուկ) *shushoog*. կկոց (կըկոց) *gugotz*.

When the liquids ն, ղ, ր, are at the end

of a syllable after another consonant, they have equally in the pronunciation the letter ը, as, *մուկն* (*մուկըն*) *moogun*. *աստղ* (*աստըղ*) *asdugh*. *դուստր* (*դուստըր*) *toosder*.

But not when they precede the consonant, as, *գունտ*, *coond*. *աղտ*, *aghd*. *կարգ*, *garck*.

Likewise when the consonants are different, as, *թուղթ*, *tooght*. *սուրբք*, *soorpk*. *հողմք*, *hoghmk*.

In the beginning of many words between two consonants the letter ը is understood in the oblique cases in stead of another vowel of the nominative case, as, *ձուկն*, *tzoogun*. *ձկան* (*ձըկան*) *tzugan*. *միշտ*, *mishd*. *մշտակայ* (*մըշտակայ*) *mushdagah*.

FAMILIAR ABBREVIATIONS

ա՟մ	ամենայն.	թ՟է or ՟է	թենէ.
ա՟յ	այսինքն.	թ՟ե or ՟ե	թեամբ.
ա՟ծ	Աստուած.	'ի վ՟ր	'ի վերայ.
ա՟յ	Աստուծոյ.	կ՟մ	կամ.
ա՟վ	Աստուծով.	Յ՟ս	Յիսուս.
բ՟զմ	բազում.	ն՟ր	նորա.
դ՟ր	դորա.	ն՟մնէ	նմանէ.
ե՟ղ	եղ.	ն՟ք	նոքա.
և	եւ.	ն՟ց	նոցա.
և՟ա	և այլն.	ն՟ս	նոսա.
ը՟դ	ընդ.	ո՟պ	որպէս.
ը՟ս	ըստ.	պ՟ս or պ՟	պէս.
թ՟ի or ՟ի	թիւն.	ս՟ր	սորա.
թ՟ե or ՟ե	թեան.	ս՟մէ	սմանէ.

սք՟	սոքա .	վն՟	վասն .
սց՟	սոցա .	վն՟յ	վասն որոյ .
սց՟է	սոցանէ .	տր՟	տէր .
ս՟բ	սուրբ .	տ՟ն	տեառն .
ս՟բյ	սրբոյ .	ք՟	քան .
ս՟բց	սրբոց .	Քս՟	Քրիստոս :

WORD

A word is an articulate sound expressive of our ideas.

Words in the Armenian language consist of eight parts of speech; Nouns, Pronouns, Verbs, Participles, Prepositions, Adverbs, Conjunctions, Interjections.

NOUN

A noun signifies some substance, or quality, as, *մարդ*, *man.* *երկիր*, *earth.* *լոյս*, *light.* *թագաւորութիւն*, *kingdom.* *հոգի*, *soul*, *spirit.* *անձն*, *person.* *բնութիւն*, *nature.* *միտք*, *mind*, *thought.* *բարի*, *good.* *գեղեցիկ*, *handsome.* *քաղցր*, *sweet.* *մեծ*, *great.*

In nouns six peculiarities are to be considered: Gender, Form, Species or Kind, Number, Case, Declension.

GENDER.

In the Armenian language the genders are distinguished by their natural significations, as

MASCULINE.

Ադամ, *Adam*. Մովսէս, *Moses*. Պետրոս, *Peter*. Գրիգոր, *Gregory*. Վարդան, *Vardan*, etc.

Հայր, *father*. եղբայր, *brother*. ուստր, *son, a male-child*. փեսայ, *a husband, spouse*. աներ, *a father-in-law*. քեռի, *uncle, a mother's brother*. կնքահայր, *gossip, Godfather*. այր, *man, husband*. ծառայ, *a man-servant*. թագաւոր or արքայ, *king*. նախարար, *satrap, a peer*. ցուլ, *a bull*. եզն, *an ox*. քաղ, *a he-goat*. խոյ, *ram, a male sheep*. զուարակ, *bullock, a young ox*. եղջերու, *a stag*. աքաղաղ, *cock*, etc.

Ատեան, *tribunal*. զօր, *soldiers*. հեծելագունդ, *cavalry, horse-troops*, etc.

FEMININE.

Եւայ, *Eve*. Սառա, *Sarah*. Մարիամ, *Mary*. Շուշան or Շուշանիկ, *Susanna*. Վարդուհի, *Rose*, etc.

Հանի, *grandmother*. մայր, *mother*. քոյր, *sister*. հարսն, *spouse, bride*. կին, *woman; wife*. դուստր, *daughter*. աղջիկ, *girl, maid*. զոքանչ, *mother-in-law*. նու, *son's wife, daughter-in-law*. սկեսուր, *mother-in-law, husband's mother*. կնքամայր, *gossip, Godmother*. դշխոյ, տիկին, թագուհի, *queen, princess*. օրիորդ, *young girl*. նաժիշտ, աղախին, *servant-maid*. կով, *cow*. երինջ, *hei-*

fer, a young cow. մաքի, *ewe, female sheep*. մարի, *hen*. եղն, *hind*, etc.

COMMON

Մարդ, *man*. որդի, զաւակ, *child*. տղայ, *infant*. ժառանգ, *an heir*. թոռն, *grandson*, or *grand-daughter*. թռչուն, *bird*. առիւծ, *lion*, or *lioness*. կորիւն, *a young beast*. ձագ, *chick, chicken*. հաւ, *bird, fowl*. ոչխար, *sheep*. արջառ, *cattle*. աղաւնի, *pigeon, dove*. ձի, *horse*. շուն, *dog, bitch*. դիւթ, *charmer*. մարգարէ, *prophet*, or *prophetess*, etc.

NEUTER

Ջուր, *water*. օդ, *air*. հող, *earth*. մարմին, *body*. երկինք, *heaven*. լոյս, *light*. ծառ, *tree*. ձեռք, *hand*. ոտք, *foot*. հոգի, *soul, spirit*. միտք, *mind*. տուն, *house*. աթոռ, *chair*. կեանք, *life*. մահ, *death*. համբերութիւն, *patience*. անիրաւութիւն, *injustice*, etc.

The genders are distinguished also in this manner: Այր մարգարէ, *prophet, a male prophet*. կին մարգարէ, *prophetess, a female prophet*. այր մարդ, *man, male*. կին մարդ, *woman*. մատակ առիւծ, *lioness, female lion, a she-lion*. արու աղաւնի, *male pigeon*. աղջիկ տղայ, *girl, a female child*, etc.

Some genders are indicated also by their terminations, as

MASCULINE.

Յովհաննէս, *John*. Յուլիանոս, *Julian*. Աթանասիոս, *Athanasius*. Թէոդորոս, *Theodore*, etc.

FEMININE.

Յովհաննա, *Joan*. Յուլիանէ, *Juliana*. Աթանասիա, *Athanasia*. Թէոդորա, *Theodora*, etc.

Վարդուհի, *Rose*. քրմուհի, *a priestess heathenish*. քահանայուհի, *a priestess*. մարգարէուհի, *a prophetess*. Աստուածուհի, *Goddess*. արքայուհի, թագուհի, տիրուհի, *queen, princess*. վկայուհի, *a she-martyr*. Աբբասուհի, *an Abbess*. Սարկաւագուհի, *Deaconess*, etc.

Վարդանոյշ, *Vard's daughter*. Սահականոյշ, *Isaac's daughter*. Խոսրովիդուխտ, *Chosroes' daughter*. Որմզդուխտ, *Hormistus' daughter*, etc.

FORM.

The forms of the nouns are three: simple, as, մարդ, *man:* Accompanied by a particle before, as, անմարդ, *inhuman:* Composed of entire words, as, մարդասէր, *human, kind*.

The different modes of producing compound epithets and words, are the treasure and ornament of the Armenian language; a thousand varieties of compounded words may be made in this tongue as may be perceived in the Armenian grammar published 1815.

SPECIES or KIND.

There are two kinds of words: Primitive, as, մարդ, *man:* and Derivative or Derived having at the termination a particle, as, մարդկային, *human*.

The Derivatives are most abundant in the Armenian language.

NUMBER.

Numbers are two: Singular, as, մարդ, *man*: and Plural, as, մարդք or մարդիկ, *men*.

The plural of some nouns is formed in a particular manner, as, կին, *woman*, կանայք, *women*. վանք, *convent*, վանորայք, վանորեայք or վանէրայք, *convents*. գիր or գիրք, *book*, գրեան, *books*. մանուկ, *child*, *boy*, մանկտի, *children*, *boys*.

The proper nouns are sometimes made plural with the particle եանք, as, Գրիգոր, *Gregory*, Գրիգորեանք, *Gregories*. Յովհաննէս, *John*, Յովհաննիսեանք, *Johns*.

CASE.

The cases in the Armenian language according to the modern authors are *ten* in number.

1. Nominative, *մարդ*, *the man.*
2. Genitive, *մարդոյ*, *of the man.*
3. Dative, *մարդոյ* or *'ի մարդ*, *to the man.*
4. Accusative, *զմարդ*, *the man.*
5. Ablative, *'ի մարդոյ*, *from the man.*
6. Narrative, *զմարդոյ*, *concerning the man.*
7. Instrumental, *մարդով*, *by means of man.*
8. Circumdative, *զմարդով*, *about the man.*
9. Commorative, *'ի մարդ* or *'ի մարդում*, *in the man.*
10. Vocative, *ով մարդ*, *o man!*

It is to be remarked in this declension that the second case is changed in the termination. The third in the termination, and is then denominated the *dative-declined-in-the-termination:* and sometimes has before it a letter or preposition, and is then called the *dative-with-the-preposition*. The fourth case has before it the letter զ, which is sometimes omitted or understood. The fifth case changes in the termination, and has the letter or preposition 'ի before it; or the letter յ when followed by a vowel. The sixth case likewise changes in the termination, and has before it the letter զ. The seventh case changes in the termination. The eighth case also, and has before it the letter զ.

The ninth case has before it the letters 'ի or յ, and when changed in the termination has always before it the same letter or preposition. The tenth case has before it the interjection ո՛ or ո՛վ, but not always expressed.

According to the ancient authors the cases are properly only six.

1. Nominative.
2. Genitive.
3. Dative.
4. Accusative.
5. Ablative.
6. Instrumental.

And these will be followed in the present grammar.

DECLENSION.

Concerning the number of declensions of the nouns the opinions of authors are various: we will reckon *ten* dividing them into two classes according to the grammar published in 1815.

The first class contains six *simple* or *regular* declensions, and the second four *mixed* or *irregular* declensions: and they are distinguished from the second and sixth cases in this manner.

REGULAR DECLENSIONS.

	SINGULAR.		PLURAL.	
	Gen.	*Instr.*	*Gen.*	*Instr.*
1.	ի,	իւ.	ից,	իւք.
2.	ի,	աւ.	աց,	աւք or օք.
3.	ոյ,	ով.	ոց,	ովք.
4.	ան,	ամբ.	անց,	ամբք.
5.	ու,	ու.	ուց,	ուք.
6.	եր,	երբ or	երց,	երբք or
	եղ,	եղբ.	եղց,	եղբք.

IRREGULAR DECLENSIONS.

	SINGULAR.		PLURAL.	
	Gen.	*Instr.*	*Gen.*	*Instr.*
1.	ւոյ,	ւով or	եաց,	ւովք or
		եաւ.	եայց,	եաւք or եօք.
2.	ին,	ամբ.	անց,	ամբք.
3.	ոջ,	աւ or ամբ.	անց,	ամբք.
4.	այ or եայ,	աւ or եաւ.		

FIRST DECLENSION.

SINGULAR.

1. Արքայ, the king.
2. Արքայի, of the king.
3. Արքայի or յարքայ, ցարքայ, to the king.
4. զԱրքայ, the king.

5. յԹագաւորէ, from the king.
6. Թագաւորաւ, with *or* by the king.

PLURAL.

1. Թագաւորք, the kings.
2. Թագաւորաց, of the kings.
3. Թագաւորաց or յԹագաւորս, ցԹագաւորս, to the kings.
4. զԹագաւորս, the kings.
5. յԹագաւորաց, from the kings.
6. Թագաւորօք, with *or* by the kings.

It may be seen by this example that the letters ք, ս, ց, form the plural; but are not always signs of the plural in the termination of a word, as, քաղաք, *city*. լոյս, *light*. հաց, *bread:* which in the plural form քաղաքք, *cities*. լոյսք, *the lights*. հացք, *the loaves.*

The third and fifth cases carry before them the letter յ, when the noun begins with a vowel, and the letter 'ի, when the noun begins with a consonant.

The cases are generally formed either by the addition of a vowel to the nominative, as, բան, *word*, բանի, *of the word*. գետ, *river*, գետոյ, *of the river*. զգեստ, *coat*, զգեստու, *of the coat*. Տրդատ, *Tiridates*, Տրդատայ, *of Tiridates:* or by placing in the termination of a word the vowel of the last syllable, as, դարբին, *workman*, դարբնի, *of the workman:* or by omitting a vowel of the last syllable, as, ատեան, *tribunal*, ատե-նի, *of the tribunal*: or by exchanging one vowel for another, as, *պարտէզ*, *garden*, *պարտիզի*, *of the garden*.

Some nouns have no singular, as, *փառք*, *glory*. *բարք*, *custom*. *դժոխք*, *hell*. *կուռք*, *idol*. *կեանք*, *life*. *երեսք*, *face*. *աղօթք*, *prayer*, etc.

And others no plural, as, *յոյս*, *hope*. *սէր*, *affection*, *love*. *քուն*, *sleep*. *երկիր*, *earth*. *ասր*, *wool*. *խաւար*, *the dark*, etc.

SECOND DECLENSION.

SINGULAR.

1. Կարգ, the order.
2. Կարգի, of the order.
3. Կարգի or 'ի կարգ, առ կարգ, to the order.
4. զԿարգ, the order.
5. 'ի Կարգէ, from the order.
6. Կարգաւ, with *or* by the order.

PLURAL.

1. Կարգք, the orders.
2. Կարգաց, of the orders.
3. Կարգաց or 'ի կարգս, to the orders.
4. զԿարգս, the orders.
5. 'ի Կարգաց, from the orders.
6. Կարգաւք or կարգօք, with *or* by the orders.

THIRD DECLENSION

SINGULAR.

1. Մարդ, the man.
2. Մարդոյ, of the man.
3. Մարդոյ or մարդուամ or 'ի մարդ, to the man.
4. զՄարդ, the man.
5. 'ի Մարդոյ, from the man.
6. Մարդով, with *or* by the man.

PLURAL.

1. Մարդք, the men.
2. Մարդոց, of the men.
3. Մարդոց or 'ի մարդս, to the men.
4. զՄարդս, the men.
5. 'ի Մարդոց, from the men.
6. Մարդովք, with *or* by the men.

FOURTH DECLENSION.

SINGULAR.

1. Հիմն, the foundation.
2. Հիմման, of the foundation.
3. Հիմման or 'ի Հիմն, to the foundation.
4. զՀիմն, the foundation.
5. 'ի Հիմմանէ, from the foundation.
6. Հիմամբ, with *or* by the foundation.

PLURAL.

1. Հիմունք, the foundations.
2. Հիմանց, of the foundations.

3. Հիմանց or 'ի հիմունս, to the foundations.
4. զՀիմունս, the foundations.
5. 'ի Հիմանց, from the foundations.
6. Հիմամբք, with *or* by the foundations.

FIFTH DECLENSION.

SINGULAR.

1. Գանձ, the treasure.
2. Գանձու, of the treasure.
3. Գանձու or 'ի գանձ, to the treasure.
4. զԳանձ, the treasure.
5. 'ի Գանձէ, from the treasure.
6. Գանձու, with *or* by the treasure.

PLURAL.

1. Գանձք, the treasures.
2. Գանձուց, of the treasures.
3. Գանձուց or 'ի գանձս, to the treasures.
4. զԳանձս, the treasures.
5. 'ի Գանձուց, from the treasures.
6. Գանձուք, with *or* by the treasures.

SIXTH DECLENSION.

SINGULAR.

1. Աղբիւր, the fountain.
2. Աղբեր, of the fountain.
3. Աղբեր or յաղբիւր, to the fountain.
4. զԱղբիւր, the fountain.

5. յԱղբերէ or յաղբիւրէ, from the fountain.
6. Աղբերբ or աղբերբաւ, with *or* by the fountain.

PLURAL.

1. Աղբերք or աղբիւրք, the fountains.
2. Աղբերց or աղբերաց, of the fountains.
3. Աղբերց, աղբերաց or յաղբերս, յաղբիւրս, to the fountains.
4. զԱղբերս or զաղբիւրս, the fountains.
5. յԱղբերց or յաղբերաց, from the fountains.
6. Աղբերբք or աղբերբաւք, with *or* by the fountains.

SEVENTH DECLENSION

SINGULAR.

1. Տեղի, the place.
2. Տեղւոյ, of the place.
3. Տեղւոյ or տեղւոջ or 'ի տեղի, to the place.
4. զՏեղի, the place.
5. 'ի Տեղւոյ or 'ի տեղւոջէ, from the place.
6. Տեղեաւ, with *or* by the place.

PLURAL.

1. Տեղիք, the places.
2. Տեղեաց, of the places.
3. Տեղեաց or 'ի տեղիս, to the places.
4. զՏեղիս, the places.

5. 'ի Տեղեաց, from the places.
6. Տեղեաւք or տեղեօք, with *or* by the places.

EIGHTH DECLENSION.

SINGULAR.

1. Բեռն, the burden.
2. Բեռին, of the burden.
3. Բեռին or 'ի բեռն, to the burden.
4. զԲեռն, the burden.
5. 'ի Բեռանէ, from the burden.
6. Բեռամբ, with *or* by the burden.

PLURAL.

1. Բեռինք, the burdens.
2. Բեռանց, of the burdens.
3. Բեռանց or 'ի բեռինս, to the burdens.
4. զԲեռինս, the burdens.
5. 'ի Բեռանց, from the burdens.
6. Բեռամբք, with *or* by the burdens.

NINTH DECLENSION.

SINGULAR.

1. Կին, the woman *or* the wife.
2. Կնոջ, of the woman.
3. Կնոջ or 'ի կին, to the woman.
4. զԿին, the woman.
5. 'ի Կնոջէ, from the woman.
6. Կնաւ or կանամբ, with *or* by the woman.

PLURAL.

1. Կանայք, the women *or* the wives.
2. Կանանց, of the women.
3. Կանանց or առ կանայս, to the women.
4. զԿանայս, the women.
5. 'ի Կանանց, from the women.
6. Կանամբք, with *or* by the women.

The following are declined in this manner.

SINGULAR.

1. Գիւղ or գեօղ, the village.
2. Գեղջ, of the village.
3. Գեղջ or 'ի գիւղ, to the village.
4. զԳիւղ, the village.
5. 'ի Գեղջէ, from the village.
6. Գիւղիւ, with *or* by the village.

PLURAL.

1. Գիւղք, the villages.
2. Գիւղից, of the villages.
3. Գիւղից or 'ի գիւղս, to the villages.
4. զԳիւղս, the villages.
5. 'ի Գիւղից, from the villages.
6. Գիւղիւք or գիւղօք, with *or* by the villages.

SINGULAR.

1. Տէր, the Lord, the Master.
2. Տեառն, of the lord.
3. Տեառն or ցտէր, to the lord.

4. զՏէր, the lord.
5. 'ի Տեառնէ or 'ի տեառնէ, from the lord.
6. Տերամբ, with *or* by the lord.

PLURAL.

1. Տեարք, the Lords, the Masters.
2. Տեարց or տերանց, of the lords.
3. Տեարց, տերանց or ցտեարս, to the lords.
4. զՏեարս, the lords.
5. 'ի Տեարց or 'ի տերանց, from the lords.
6. Տերամբք, with *or* by the lords.

SINGULAR.

1. Աւր or օր, the day.
2. Աւուր, of the day.
3. Աւուր or յաւուր or յօր, to the day.
4. զԱւր or զօր, the day.
5. յԱւրէ or յօրէ, from the day.
6. Աւուրբ, with *or* by the day.

PLURAL.

1. Աւուրք, the days.
2. Աւուրց, of the days.
3. Աւուրց or յաւուրս, to the days.
4. զԱւուրս, the days.
5. յԱւուրց, from the days.
6. Աւուրբք, with *or* by the days.

SINGULAR.

1. Հայր, the father.
2. Հաւր or Հօր, of the father.
3. Հաւր, Հօր or ցՀայր, to the father.

4. զՀայր, the father.
5. 'ի Հաւրէ or 'ի հօրէ, from the father.
6. Հարբ, with *or* by the father.

PLURAL.

1. Հարք, the fathers.
2. Հարց or հարանց, of the fathers.
3. Հարց, հարանց or ցհարս, to the fathers.
4. զՀարս, the fathers.
5. 'ի Հարց or 'ի հարանց, from the fathers.
6. Հարբք, with *or* by the fathers.

TENTH DECLENSION.

SINGULAR.

1. Տիգրան, Tigranes.
2. Տիգրանայ, of Tigranes.
3. Տիգրանայ or 'ի Տիգրան, to Tigranes.
4. զՏիգրան, Tigranes.
5. 'ի Տիգրանայ, from Tigranes.
6. Տիգրանաւ, with *or* by Tigranes.

SINGULAR.

1. Հեղինէ, Helena.
2. Հեղինեայ, of Helena.
3. Հեղինեայ or առ Հեղինէ, to Helena.
4. զՀեղինէ, Helena.
5. 'ի Հեղինեայ, from Helena.
6. Հեղինեաւ, with *or* by Helena.

ADJECTIVE

An Adjective is a word added to a Substantive to express its quality.

Adjectives in the Armenian language admit besides the number or case the degrees of comparison.

The Comparatives are formed in three modes; 1. with the particle գոյն, as *բարի, good, բարեգոյն, better. չար, bad, չարագոյն, worse. բազում, much, many, բազմագոյն, more.* 2. with the prepositions քան, ևս, առաւել as, *մեծ, great, մեծ քան, մեծ ևս, առաւել մեծ, greater.* 3. with different cases of the substantive, as, *մեծն մարգարէից, greater than all prophets. մեծն 'ի մարգարէս, greater amongst the prophets.*

The Superlatives are also formed in three manners: 1. with the particles ամէն or ամեն, գեր, մեծ, երեք or եռ put before them, as, *ամենաբարի, best. ամենիմաստուն, wisest. գերամաքուր, most clean. մեծավայելուչ, most convenient. եռամեծ, greatest.* 2. by adding to them some adverbs, as, *ևս մեծագոյն* or *մեծագոյն ևս, greatest. յոյժ վատթարագոյն, ամենահնարին չար, worst. ամենեւին գեղեցիկ, most handsome. երիցս եղկելի, most miserable.* 3. by redoubling the positives, as, *մեծամեծ, greatest. չարաչար* or *չար առաւել քան զչար, worst.*

MIDDLE NOUNS

Those nouns are named *middle* or *mixed*, which are neither Substantives nor Pronouns, and are classed generally in English among the Adjectives.

They are of five kinds: Numeral, Partitive, General, Interrogative, and Relative.

THE NOUNS NUMERAL.

The nouns numeral are of five kinds: Absolute, Cardinal, Separative, Distributive, and Replicative.

ABSOLUTE.

Մի or *մին*, *մու*, *եզ*, *one.*
Երկու, *two.*
Երեք or *եռ*, *երր*, *three.*
Չորք or *չորս*, *four.*
Հինգ, *five.*
Վեց, *six.*
Եւթն or *եօթն*, *seven.*
Ութ, *eight.*
Ինն, *nine.*
Տասն, *ten.*
Մետասան, *eleven.*
Երկոտասան, *twelve.*
Երեքտասան, *thirteen.*
Չորեքտասան, *fourteen.*
Հնգետասան, *fifteen.*
Վեշտասան, *sixteen.*

Եւթնևտասն or եւթնուտասն, *seventeen.*
Ութևտասն or ութուտասն, *eighteen.*
Իննևտասն or իննուտասն, *nineteen.*
Քսան, *twenty.*
Քսան և մի, *twenty one.*
Երեսուն, *thirty.*
Երեսուն և երկու, *thirty two.*
Քառասուն, *forty.*
Քառասուն և երեք, *forty three.*
Յիսուն, *fifty.*
Յիսուն և չորք, *fifty four.*
Վաթսուն, *sixty.*
Եւթանասուն, *seventy.*
Ութսուն, *eighty.*
Իննսուն, *ninety.*
Իննսուն և ինն, *ninety nine.*
Հարիւր, *hundred.*
Երկերիւր, *two hundred.*
Երեքհարիւր, *three hundred.*
Չորեքհարիւր, *four hundred.*
Հինգհարիւր, *five hundred.*
Վեցհարիւր, *six hundred.*
Եւթնհարիւր, *seven hundred.*
Ութհարիւր, *eight hundred.*
Իննհարիւր, *nine hundred.*
Հազար, *thousand.*
Բեւր or բիւր, *ten thousand.*

CARDINAL.

Առաջին or առաջնորդ, առաջներորդ, նախկին, նախնի, *first.*
Երկրորդ, *second.*

Երրորդ or երիր, *third.*
Չորրորդ or չորիր, քառորդ, *fourth.*
Հինգերորդ, *fifth.*
Վեցերորդ, *sixth.*
Եւթներորդ, *seventh.*
Ութերորդ, *eighth.*
Իններորդ, *ninth.*
Տասներորդ, *tenth.*
Քսաներորդ, *twentieth.*
Երեսներորդ, *thirtieth.*
Քառասներորդ, *fortieth.*
Յիսներորդ, *fiftieth.*
Վաթսներորդ, *sixtieth.*
Եւթանասներորդ, *seventieth.*
Ութսներորդ, *eightieth.*
Իննսներորդ, *ninetieth.*
Հարիւրերորդ or Հարիւրորդ, *hundredth.*
Երկերիւրերորդ, *two hundredth.*
Հազարերորդ, *thousandth.*

SEPARATIVE.

Միակ, *one, sole, only.*
Երկեակ or երկակ, *two only, two.*
Երրեակ, *three only, three.*
Չորեակ or քառեակ, *four only, four.*
Հնգեակ, *five only, five.*
Տասնեակ, *ten only, ten.*
Եւթանասնեակ, *seventy only, seventy.*
Հարիւրեակ, *hundred only, hundred.*

DISTRIBUTIVE.

Երկոքեան or *երկոքին*, *both, the two.*
Երեքեան or *երեքին*, *the three.*
Չորեքեան or *չորեքին*, *the four.*
Եւթանեքեան or *եւթանեքին*, *the seven.*
Երկոտասանեքեան or *երկոտասանեքին*, *the twelve.*

Երկաքանչիւր, *both, one and the other.*

REPLICATIVE.

Երկպատիկ or *կրկին*, *double, two.*
Երեքպատիկ, *եռապատիկ* or *երեքկին*, *triple, treble, threefold.*
Չորեքպատիկ, *քառապատիկ* or *չորեքկին*, *fourfold.*
Հնգապատիկ, *quintuple, fivefold.*
Եւթնապատիկ, *sevenfold.*
Տասնպատիկ, *tenfold.*
Հարիւրապատիկ, *hundredfold.*
Հազարապատիկ, *thousandfold.*

THE NOUNS PARTITIVE.

Ոմն, ոք, իք, *some, somebody, one, any, whosoever.*

Իմն, *ինչ*, *a, one, some, certain, single, any.*
Միմեանց or *իրերաց*, *of one, of the other.*
Իւրաքանչիւր or *անցնիւր*, *each, every, any.*
Մեւս or *միւս*, *other, another.*
Այլ ոք, *այլ ոմն*, *another.*
Այլ իմն, *այլ ինչ*, *another, different.*

Մ՛իւս ոմն, *another.*
Իւրաքանչիւր ոք, *every one.*
Իւրաքանչիւր ինչ, *every* or *any thing.*
Մ՛ի մի, *every, any.*
Քանի ինչ or քանի մի, *some, not many.*

THE NOUNS GENERAL.

Ամենայն or ամէն, *all, every, any.*
Ամենեքեան or ամենեքին, *all, every one.*
Բոլոր, *all, whole, entire, total.*
Բոլորեքեան or բոլորեքին, *all, every one.*
Համայն, համակ, համօրէն, բնաւ, ողջոյն, *all, whole, entire, total, complete.*
Ամենայն ոք, *every one.*
Ամենայն ինչ, *every* or *any thing.*
Որ ոք, *whoever, whosoever.*
Որ ինչ, *whatsoever.*
Ոչ ոք, *none, not one, not any, nobody.*
Ոչ ինչ or ոչ մի ինչ, *nothing, not any thing.*

THE NOUNS INTERROGATIVE.

Ո՞ or ո՞վ, *who? which person?*
Ո՞ր, *who? which?*
Ի՞նչ, *what? which?*
Քանի՞, *how much? how many?*
Ո՞վ ոք, ո՞ ոք, ո՞ր ոք, *whoever? who?*
Ո՞ր իմն, զի՞նչ ինչ, *whatever? what?*
Ո՞րպիսի, զի՞նչպիսի, *what? which?*
Ո՞րքան, ո՞րչափ, *how much? how many?*

Ն. *այսպիսի, սոյնպիսի, such, like, same, similar, as, so.*
Ն. *այդպիսի, դոյնպիսի, so, as, like, similar.*
Ն. *այնպիսի, նոյնպիսի, so, as, as that, like that.*
Ն. *այսքան, սոյնքան, so much, as many.*
Ն. *այսչափ, սոյնչափ, so much, as many.*
Ն. *այդքան, դոյնքան, so many, so much.*
Ն. *այդչափ, դոյնչափ, so many, so much.*
Ն. *այնքան, նոյնքան, so many, so much.*
Ն. *այնչափ, նոյնչափ, so many, so much, so much as.*

All these middle nouns are declined under one of the ten declensions of nouns substantive, except ոմն and ոք, which are differently declined in the singular, but similarly in the plural number, as

SINGULAR.

1.	Ոմն, one, some.	Ոք, one, any person.
2.	Ուրումն, of one.	Ուրուք, of any.
3.	Ումեմն, to one.	Ումեք, to any.
4.	զՈմն, one.	զՈք, any.
5.	յՈւմեմնէ, from one.	յՈւմեքէ, from any.
6.	Ոմամբ, with *or* by one.	Ոմամբ, with *or* by any.

PLURAL.

1. Ոմանք, some.
2. Ոմանց, of some.
3. Ոմանց or յոմանս, ցոմանս, to some.
4. զՈմանս, some.
5. յՈմանց, from some.
6. Ոմամբք, with *or* by some.

PRONOUN

Pronouns stand in place of nouns and, like them, have case, number, and particularly the first, second and third persons, as, *ես, I. դու, thou. նա, he.*

In Armenian they have no genders.

There are four kinds of pronouns: Substantive or Personal, as, *ես, I. դու, thou. ինքն, he, himself. իւր, own, himself.* Definitive, as, *սա, this* (person or thing). *դա, that* (person or thing). *նա, that, he, she, it.* Possessive, as, *իմ* or *իմոյին, my, mine. մեր* or *մերոյին, our, our's. քո* or *քոյին, thy, thine. ձեր* or *ձերոյին, your, your's. իւր* or *իւրայ-ին, his, hers, its. իւրեանց, their, their's.* And Relative, as, *որ, who, which, that, what.*

The three letters *ս, դ, ն,* are called Articles-distinctive-of-the-persons; and, joined to the terminations of words and verbs, shew their persons or order, and are used as pronouns personal, possessive, and definitive, as, *մարդս, I who am a man,* or *my man,* or *this* man. մարդդ, *thou who art a man*, or *thy man*, or *that man*. մարդն, *he who is a man*, or *his man* or *that man*.

DECLENSIONS OF THE PERSONAL PRONOUNS.

1. *Person.*

SINGULAR.

1. Ես, I.
2. Իմ, of me, mine *or* my.
3. Ինձ, ցիս, առ իս, to me.
4. զԻս, me.
5. յԻնէն, from me.
6. Ինեւ, with *or* by me.

PLURAL.

1. Մեք, we.
2. Մեր, of us, our *or* our's.
3. Մեզ, ցմեզ, առ մեզ, to us.
4. զՄեզ, us.
5. 'ի Մէնջ, from us.
6. Մեւք or մեօք, with *or* by us.

2. *Person.*

SINGULAR.

1. Դու, thou.
2. Քո, of thee, thine *or* thy.
3. Քեզ, առ քեզ, ցքեզ, to thee.
4. զՔեզ, thee.
5. 'ի Քէն, from thee.
6. Քեւ, with *or* by thee.

PLURAL.

1. Դուք, ye *or* you.
2. Ձեր, of you, your *or* your's.
3. Ձեզ, ցձեզ, առ ձեզ, to you.
4. զՁեզ, you.
5. 'ի Ձէնջ, from you.
6. Ձեւք or ձեօք, with *or* by you.

3. *Person.*

SINGULAR.

1. Ինքն, he *or* himself.
2. Ինքեան, of him *or* his.
3. Ինքեան or առ ինքն, to him.
4. զԻնքն, him.
5. յԻնքենէ, from him.
6. Ինքեամբ, with *or* by him.

PLURAL.

1. Ինքեանք, they *or* themselves.
2. Ինքեանց, of them, their *or* their's.
3. Ինքեանց or առ ինքեանս, to them.
4. զԻնքեանս, them.
5. յԻնքեանց, from them.
6. Ինքեամբք, with *or* by them.

Ինքն alone signifies *he, she,* but accompanied by another pronoun signifies *self,* as, *ես ինքն, myself. դու ինքն, thyself. նա ինքն, himself.*

SINGULAR.

1.
2. Իւր or իւրեան, his.
3. Իւր, իւրեան or առ իւր, to him, to himself.
4.
5. յԻւրմէ, from him, from himself.
6. Իւրեւ, իւրեաւ or իւրեամբ, with *or* by him *or* himself.

PLURAL.

1.
2. Իւրեանց, their, their's.
3. Իւրեանց, to them *or* to themselves.
4.
5. յԻւրեանց, from them, from themselves.
6. Իւրեամբք, with *or* by them *or* themselves.

Declension of Definitive Pronouns Personal.

1. *Person.*

SINGULAR.

1. Սա, this (person).
2. Սորա, of this.
3. Սմա or առ սա, to this.
4. զՍա, this.
5. 'ի Սմանէ, from this.
6. Սովաւ, with *or* by this.

PLURAL.

1. Սոքա, these (persons).
2. Սոցա, of these.
3. Սոցա or առ սոսա, to these.
4. զՍոսա, these.
5. 'ի Սոցանէ, from these.
6. Սոքաւք or սոքօք, by *or* with these.

2. *Person.*

SINGULAR.

1. Դա, that (person).
2. Դորա, of that.
3. Դմա or ցդա, to that.
4. զԴա, that.
5. 'ի Դմանէ, from that.
6. Դովաւ, by *or* with that.

PLURAL.

1. Դոքա, those (persons).
2. Դոցա, of those.
3. Դոցա or առ դոսա, to those.
4. զԴոսա, those.
5. 'ի Դոցանէ, from those.
6. Դոքաւք or դոքօք, by *or* with those.

3. *Person.*

SINGULAR.

1. Նա, that (person) he, she.
2. Նորա, of that.

3. Նմա or ցնա, առ նա, to that.
4. զՆա, that.
5. 'ի Նմանէ, from that.
6. Նովաւ, by *or* with that.

PLURAL.

1. Նոքա, those.
2. Նոցա, of those.
3. Նոցա or առ նոսա, ցնոսա, to those.
4. զՆոսա, those.
5. 'ի Նոցանէ, from those.
6. Նոքաւք or նոքօք, by *or* with those.

Declensions of Definitive Pronouns Adjective.

1. *Person.*

SINGULAR.

1. Այս, this (person *or* thing).
2. Այսր or այսորիկ, of this.
3. Այսմ, այսմիկ or առ այս, to this.
4. զԱյս, this.
5. յԱյսմանէ, from this.
6. Այսու or այսուիկ, by *or* with this.

PLURAL.

1. Այսք or այսոքիկ, these.
2. Այսց or այսոցիկ, of these.
3. Այսց, այսոցիկ or առ այսոսիկ, to these.
4. զԱյսոսիկ, these.
5. յԱյսց or յայսցանէ, from these.
6. Այսոքիւք or այսոքիմբք, by *or* with these.

2. *Person.*

SINGULAR.

1. Այդ, that (person *or* thing).
2. Այդր or *այդորիկ*, of that.
3. Այդմ, *այդմիկ* or *առ այդ*, to that.
4. զԱյդ, that.
5. յԱյդմանէ, from that.
6. Այդու or *այդուիկ*, by *or* with that.

PLURAL.

1. Այդք or *այդոքիկ*, those.
2. Այդց or *այդոցիկ*, of those.
3. Այդց, *այդոցիկ* or *առ այդոսիկ*, to those.
4. զԱյդոսիկ, those.
5. յԱյդց or *յայդցանէ*, from those.
6. Այդոքիւք or *այդոքիմբք*, by *or* with those.

3. *Person.*

SINGULAR.

1. Այն, that (person *or* thing).
2. Այնր or *այնորիկ*, of that.
3. Այնմ, *այնմիկ* or *առ այն*, to that.
4. զԱյն, that.
5. յԱյնմանէ, from that.
6. Այնու or *այնուիկ*, by *or* with that.

PLURAL.

1. Այնք or *այնոքիկ*, those.
2. Այնց or *այնոցիկ*, of those.

3. *Այնց, այնոցիկ* or *առ այնոսիկ, յայնս,* to those.
4. *զԱյնոսիկ* or *զայնս,* those.
5. *յԱյնց* or *յայնցանէ,* from those.
6. *Այնոքիւք* or *այնոքիմբք* , by *or* with those.

Other Definitive Pronouns Adjective.

1. *Person.*

SINGULAR.

1. *Սոյն,* this same (person *or* thing).
2. *Սորին* or *սորուն,* of this same.
3. *Սմին* or *առ սոյն,* to this same.
4. *զՍոյն,* this same.
5. ('*ի Սոյն* or '*ի սմին*) from this same.
6. *Սովին* or *սովիմբ,* by *or* with this same.

PLURAL.

1. *Սոյնք* or *սոքին,* these same.
2. *Սոցին, սոցուն* or *սոցունց,* of these same.
3. *Սոցին* or *առ սոսին, առ սոյնս,* to these same.
4. *զՍոյնս, զսոսին,* these same.
5 '*ի Սոցունց,* from these same.
6. *Սովիմբք* , *սոքիմբք* or *սոքումբք,* by *or* with these same.

2. *Person.*

SINGULAR.

1. Դոյն, that same (person *or* thing) .
2. Դորին or դորուն, of that same.
3. Դմին or առ դոյն, to that same.
4. զԴոյն, that same.
5. ('ի Դոյն or 'ի դմին) from that same.
6. Դովին or դովիմբ, by *or* with that same.

PLURAL.

1. Դոյնք or դոքին, those same.
2. Դոցին, դոցուն or դոցունց, of those same.
3. Դոցին or առ դոսին, առ դոյնս, to those same.
4. զԴոյնս or զդոսին, those same.
5. 'ի Դոցունց, from those same.
6. Դովիմբք, դոքիմբք or դոքումբք, by *or* with those same.

3. *Person.*

SINGULAR.

1. Նոյն, that same (person *or* thing).
2. Նորին or նորուն, of that same.
3. Նմին or առ նոյն, to that same.
4. զՆոյն, that same.
5. ('ի Նոյն or 'ի նմին) from that same.
6. Նովին or նովիմբ, by *or* with that same.

PLURAL.

1. Նոյնք or նոքին, those same.
2. Նոցին, նոցուն or նոցունց, of those same.
3. Նոցին or առ նոսին, առ նոյնս, to those same.
4. զՆոյնս or զնոսին, those same.
5. ’ի Նոցունց, from those same.
6. Նովիմբք, նոքիմբք or նոքումբք, by *or* with those same.

The Definitive pronouns are accompanied sometimes with the pronoun *ինքն*, *self*, as, *սա ինքն*, *this self-same*. *դա ինքն*, *that self-same* or *himself*. *նա ինքն*, *that self-same* or *himself*. *այս ինքն*, *this same*. *նոյն ինքն*, *same*, *that same*.

Or they are joined together, as, *սոյն սա*, *this same*. *դոյն դա*, *դոյն այդ*, *that same*, *the same*, *himself*.

Declensions of Pronouns Possessive.

The Possessive pronouns are formed of personal and definitive pronouns; the second case of these forms the first case of the possessive.

1. *Person.*

SINGULAR.

1. Իմ, my (mine).
2. Իմոյ, of my.

3. Իմում or առ իմ, to my.
4. զԻմ, my.
5. յԻմմէ or յիմոյ, from my.
6. Իմով, by *or* with my.

PLURAL.

1. Իմք, my.
2. Իմոց, of my.
3. Իմոց, առ իմն, to my.
4. զԻմն, my.
5. յԻմոց, from my.
6. Իմովք, by *or* with my.

SINGULAR.

1. Մեր, our.
2. Մերոյ, of our, our's.
3. Մերում, to our.
4. զՄեր, our.
5. 'ի Մերմէ or 'ի մերոյ, from our.
6. Մերով, by *or* with our.

PLURAL.

1. Մերք, our.
2. Մերոց, of our.
3. Մերոց, to our.
4. զՄերս, our.
5. 'ի Մերոց, from our.
6. Մերովք, by *or* with our.

2. *Person.*

SINGULAR.

1. Քո, thy (thine).
2. Քոյ, of thy.
3. Քոյ or քում, to thy.
4. զՔո, thy.
5. 'ի Քումմէ or 'ի քոյ, from thy.
6. Քով, by *or* with thy.

PLURAL.

1. Քոյք, thy.
2. Քոց, of thy.
3. Քոց or 'ի քոյս, to thy.
4. զՔոյս, thy.
5. 'ի Քոց, from thy.
6. Քովք, by *or* with thy.

SINGULAR.

1. Ձեր, your.
2. Ձերոյ, of your, your's.
3. Ձերում, to your.
4. զՁեր, your.
5. 'ի Ձերմէ or 'ի ձերոյ, from your.
6. Ձերով, by *or* with your.

PLURAL.

1. Ձերք, your.
2. Ձերոց, of your.
3. Ձերոց, to your.
4. զՁերս, your.
5. 'ի Ձերոց, from your.
6. Ձերովք, by *or* with your.

3. *Person.*

SINGULAR.

1. Իւր, his *or* her.
2. Իւրոյ, of his.
3. Իւրում, to his.
4. զԻւր, his.
5. յԻւրմէ or յիւրոյ, from his.
6. Իւրով, by *or* with his.

PLURAL.

1. Իւրք, his.
2. Իւրոց, of his.
3. Իւրոց, to his.
4. զԻւրս, his.
5. յԻւրոց, from his.
6. Իւրովք, by *or* with his.

From the genitives of these are formed other possessives with a particle ին; they have the same signification, but are declined with prepositions, and are these: *իմոյին*, *my, mine*. *քոյին*, *thy, thine*. *մերոյին*, *our*. *ձերոյին*, *your*. *իւրոյին*, *his* or *her own*.

The same possessives are formed also in this manner: *իմային*, *my, mine*. *մերային*, *our*. *ձերային*, *your*. *իւրային*, *his*. *իւրեանցային*, *their*: and these are declined.

Declensions of Possessives derived from the Definitives.

1. *Person.*

SINGULAR.

1. Սորա, his *or* her.
2. Սորայոյ, of his.
3. Սորայում, to his.
4.
5.
6. Սորայով, by *or* with his.

PLURAL.

1. Սորայք, his *or* her.
2. Սորայց or *սորայոց*, of his.
3. Սորայց or *սորայոց*, to his.
4. զՍորայս, his.
5. 'ի Սորայոց, from his.
6. Սորայովք, by *or* with his.

SINGULAR.

1. Սոցա, their.
2. Սոցայոյ, of their.
3. Սոցայում, to their.
4.
5.
6. Սոցայով, by *or* with their.

PLURAL.

1. Սոցայք, their.
2. Սոցայց or *սոցայոց*, of their.

3. Սոցայց or սոցայոց, to their.
4. զՍոցայս, their.
5. 'ի Սոցայոց, from their.
6. Սոցայովք, by *or* with their.

2. *Person.*

SINGULAR.

1. Նորայ, his *or* her.
2. Նորայոյ, of his.
3. Նորայում, to his.
4.
5.
6. Նորայով, by *or* with his.

PLURAL.

1. Նորայք, his *or* her.
2. Նորայց or նորայոց, of his.
3. Նորայց, նորայոց or 'ի նորայս, to his.
4. զՆորայս, his.
5. 'ի Նորայոց, from his.
6. Նորայովք, by *or* with his.

SINGULAR.

1. Նոցա, their.
2. Նոցայոյ, of their.
3. Նոցայում, to their.
4.
5.
6. Նոցայով, by *or* with their.

PLURAL.

1. Դոցայք, their.
2. Դոցայց or դոցայոց, of their.
3. Դոցայոց or 'ի դոցայս, to their.
4. զԴոցայս, their.
5. 'ի Դոցայոց, from their.
6. Դոցայովք, by *or* with their.

3. *Person.*

SINGULAR.

1. Նորա, his *or* her.
2. Նորայոյ, of his.
3. Նորայում, to his.
4.
5.
6. Նորայով, by *or* with his.

PLURAL.

1. Նորայք, his *or* her.
2. Նորայց or նորայոց, of his.
3. Նորայց, նորայոց or 'ի նորայս, to his.
4. զՆորայս, his.
5. 'ի Նորայոց, from his.
6. Նորայովք, by *or* with his.

SINGULAR.

1. Նոցա, their.
2. Նոցայոյ, of their.
3. Նոցայում, to their.
4.
5.
6. Նոցայով, by *or* with their.

PLURAL.

1. Նոցայք, their.
2. Նոցայց or նոցայոց, of their.
3. Նոցայոց or ՚ի Նոցայս, to their.
4. զՆոցայս, their.
5. ՚ի Նոցայոց, from their.
6. Նոցայովք, by *or* with their.

Declension of the Pronoun Relative.

SINGULAR.

1. Որ or ո, who, which, what, that.
2. Որոյ, whose, of which.
3. Որում or առ որ, to whom, to which.
4. զՈր, whom.
5. յՈրմէ or յորոյ, from whom, from which.
6. Որով, with *or* by whom *or* which.

PLURAL.

1. Որք, who, which, what, that.
2. Որոց, whose, of which.
3. Որոց or առ որս, to which.
4. զՈրս, which.
5. յՈրոց, from which.
6. Որովք, by *or* with which.

VERB

The verb signifies to be, to do, or to suffer with tense, number and person.

Five properties belong to the verb. Kind,

Tense *or* Time, Number, Person and Conjugation.

KIND.

There are four kinds of verbs: Substantive, Active, Passive, and Neutral.

The first denotes existence, as, եմ, *I am*. գոմ, *I do exist*. The second action, as, առնեմ, *I do, I make*. The third sufferance, as, առնիմ, *I am done* or *made*. The fourth the action subsisting in itself, as, աշխատիմ, *I labour*. գնամ, *I go*.

There is also another kind called Common, which signifies the action as well as the sufferance, as, դատիմ, *I judge*, and *I am judged*.

TENSE.

There are three tenses of the verb: the Present, as, գրեմ, *I write*. Past, as, գրեցի, *I wrote*: and Future, as, գրեցից, *I shall write*.

The past is either Imperfect, as, գրէի, *I was writing*, or Perfect, as, գրեցի, *I wrote*.

The ancient grammarians add two other perfect tenses: the Preter-perfect, as, գրեալ եմ, *I have written*, and the Preter-plu-perfect, as, գրեալ էի, *I had written:* but these tenses do not necessarily belong to the Armenian language.

NUMBER.

The verb has two numbers: Singular, as, գրեմ, *I write*, and Plural, as, գրեմք, *we write*.

PERSON.

The persons are three: First, as, գրեմ, *I write*. Second, as, գրես, *thou writest.* and Third, as, գրէ, *he writes.*

CONJUGATION.

The variation of a verb in it's tenses, numbers, and persons is called conjugation.

Conjugation is either Regular or Irregular.

Regular conjugation changes regularly in the termination of the verb without any omission.

The irregular conjugation wants some tense or mood, and is called *Defective*; or in some tense or mood deviates from the rule, and is called *Devious*; or wants the first and second person, and is called *Impersonal.*

MOODS OF THE VERB.

The manner of signifying some action is called the Mood. There are four in the regular verbs: Indicative, Imperative, Subjunctive and Infinitive.

When the verb indicates some action, affirming it simply, it is called the indicative, as, *գրեմ*, *I write*. *գրեցի*, *I wrote*· *գրեցից*, *I shall write*.

When it commands or prohibits, it is called imperative, as, *գրեա*, *write thou* or *do thou write*. *մի գրեր*, *do thou write not*.

When it expresses a suspended action, or dependent upon another verb to complete the sense, it is called subjunctive, as, *եթէ գրիցեմ*, *if I write*.

When one action is denoted without tense, number or person, the mood is called infinitive, as, *գրել*, *to write*.

The indicative has three tenses, with persons and numbers. The imperative has two tenses: present, and future; it has two numbers, but in the singular has no first person, because he who speaks does not command himself. However in the plural there is a first person, because other persons are addressed and commanded.

The subjunctive has the numbers, and persons perfect: but in the tenses has only the present, and the future, because the Armenian language has not properly the past tense of subjunctive.

The infinitive has neither tense, number, nor person: whence it is used as a noun, and declined in the singular, and is then called the Gerund.

Example.

SINGULAR.

1. Գրել, to write.
2. Գրելոյ, of writing.
3. Գրելոյ or 'ի գրել, to writing.
4. զԳրել, the writing.
5. 'ի Գրելոյ, from writing.
6. Գրելով, with *or* by writing, writing.

The Conjugations of the verbs are four, and are distinguished by the last vowels of their indicatives, which are, ե, ա, ու, ի.

The indicative of the first conjugation ends with the vowel ե, as, *շարժեմ*, *I move*; of the second with ա, as, *լուանամ*, *I wash*; of the third with ու, as, *հեղում*, *I pour out*; of the fourth with ի, as, *ուսանիմ*, *I learn*.

Every conjugation although different in its moods, tenses, numbers and persons, preserves the first syllable of it's indicative, excepting such verbs as are Devious.

Every person and tense of the verb ending in ք or ն, is plural. ք is the sign of the first and second person, and ն of the third; provided only that ն be not the article distinctive of the person, because it then would be singular.

Every verb which terminates in մ, is in the first person; in ս, is in the second person; verbs ending in է or յ, are in the first or second person; verbs ending in է, աւ, ու, այ or ան, in the third person; and those terminating in ր, are in the second and third person.

In every conjugation the future of the indicative is formed by adding the letter ց to the perfect, as, *շարժեցի, I moved, շարժեցից, I shall move. լուացի, I washed, լուացից, I shall wash. հեղի, I poured out, հեղից, I shall pour out. ուսայ, I learned, ուսայց, I shall learn.*

PARTICIPLE

The participle is formed by adding to the termination of the verb the particles ող or օղ (sign of the present), եալ (sign of the past), լոց or լի (sign of the future).

As a verb it has tense, and as a noun, cases and numbers.

Example.

PRESENT.

Singular.

1. Գ՚րող or գրօղ, he who writes, *or* is writing.
2. Գ՚րողի, of him who writes.
3. Գ՚րողի or առ գրողն, to him who writes.
4. զԳ՚րող, him who writes.

5. 'ի Գրողէ, from him who writes.
6. Գրողաւ, by *or* with him who writes.

Plural.

1. Գրողք, those who write, *or* who are writing.
2. Գրողաց, of those who write.
3. Գրողաց or առ գրողս, to those who write.
4. զԳրողս, those who write.
5. 'ի Գրողաց, from those who write.
6. Գրողաւք or գրողօք, by *or* with those who write.

PAST.

Singular.

1. Գրեալ, written *or* wrote.
2. Գրելոյ, of written.
3. Գրելոյ or առ գրեալն, to written.
4. զԳրեալն, written.
5. 'ի Գրելոյ, from written.
6. Գրելով, by *or* with written.

Plural.

1. Գրեալք, written *or* wrote.
2. Գրելոց, of written.
3. Գրելոց or առ գրեալս, to written.
4. զԳրեալս, written.
5. 'ի Գրելոց, from written.
6. Գրելովք, by *or* with written.

FUTURE.

The future ending in ոց, is declined only with prepositions, as,

Singular.

1. Գրելոց, to be written.
3. 'ի Գրելոց, to that to be written.
4. զԳրելոց, to be written.

Plural.

1. Գրելոցք, to be written.
3. 'ի Գրելոցս, to that to be written.
4. զԳրելոցս, to be written.

The future terminated in ելի, is declined thus,

Singular.

1. Գրելի, to be written.
2. Գրելւոյ, of that to be written.
3. Գրելւոյ or առ գրելի, to that to be written.
4. զԳրելի, to be written.
5. 'ի Գրելւոյ, from that to be written.
6. Գրելեաւ, by *or* with that to be written.

Plural.

1. Գրելիք, to be written.
2. Գրելեաց, of that to be written.
3. Գրելեաց or 'ի գրելիս, to that to be written.
4. զԳրելիս, to be written.

5. Ի Գրելեայ, from that to be written.
6. Գրելեաւք or գրելեօք, by *or* with that to be written.

Specimen of the four conjugations of the verbs regular with their moods, tenses, numbers and persons.

INDICATIVE.

Present.

	Sing. Pers.	*Plur. Pers.*
1.	Շարժ-եմ-ես-է.	եմք-էք-են.
2.	Լուան-ամ-աս-այ.	ամք-այք-ան.
3.	Հեղ-ում-ուս-ու.	ումք-ուք-ուն.
4.	Ուսան-իմ-իս-ի.	իմք-իք-ին.

Imperfect.

1.	Շարժ-էի-էիր-էր.	էաք-էիք-էին.
2.	Լուան-այի-այիր-այր.	այաք-այիք-ային.
3.	Հեղ-ուի-ուիր-ույր.	ուաք-ուիք-ուին.
4.	Ուսան-էի-էիր-էր.	էաք-էիք-էին.

Perfect.

1.	Շարժ-եցի-եցեր-եաց.	եցաք-եցիք-եցին.
2.	Լուա-ցի-ցեր-լուաց.	ցաք-ցիք-ցին.
3.	Հեղ-ի-եր-հեղ.	աք-իք-ին.
4.	Ուս-այ-ար-աւ.	աք-այք-ան.

Future.

1	Շարժ-եցից-եսցես-եսցէ.	եսցուք-եսջիք-եսցեն.
2.	Լուա-ցից-սցես-սցէ.	սցուք-սջիք-սցեն.
3.	Հեղ-ից-ցես-ցէ.	ցուք-ջիք-ցեն.
4.	Ուս-այց-ցիս-ցի.	ցուք-ջիք-ցին.

IMPERATIVE.

Present.

1. Շարժեա՛, մի՛ շարժեր.	Շարժեցէ՛ք, մի՛ շարժէք.
Շարժեսցէ՛, մի՛ շարժեսցէ.	Շարժեսցե՛ն, մի՛ շարժեսցեն.
2. Լուա՛, մի՛ լուանար.	Լուացէ՛ք, մի՛ լուանայք.
Լուասցէ՛, մի՛ լուասցէ.	Լուասցե՛ն, մի՛ լուասցեն.
3. Հե՛ղ, մի՛ հեղուր.	Հեղէ՛ք, մի՛ հեղուք.
Հեղցէ՛, մի՛ հեղցէ.	Հեղցե՛ն, մի՛ հեղցեն.
4. Ուսի՛ր, մի՛ ուսանիր.	Ուսարո՛ւք, մի՛ ուսանիք.
Ուսցի՛, մի՛ ուսցի.	Ուսցի՛ն, մի՛ ուսցին.

Future.

1. Շարժեսջի՛ր or շարժեսցես, շարժեսցէ՛.	Շարժեսցո՛ւք, շարժեսջի՛ք, շարժեսցե՛ն.
2. Լուասջի՛ր or լուասցես, լուասցէ՛.	Լուացո՛ւք, լուասջի՛ք, լուասցե՛ն.
3. Հեղջի՛ր or հեղցես, հեղցէ՛.	Հեղցո՛ւք, հեղջի՛ք, հեղցե՛ն.
4. Ուսջի՛ր or ուսանիջի՛ր, ուսցի՛.	Ուսցո՛ւք, ուսջի՛ք or ուսանիջի՛ք, ուսցի՛ն.

SUBJUNCTIVE.

The present is formed like that of indicative.

Future.

1. Շարժ-եցեմ-եցես-եցէ.	եցեմք-եցէք-եցեն.
2. Լուան-այցեմ-այցես-այցէ.	այցեմք-այցէք-այցեն.
3. Հեղ-ուցում-ուցուս-ուցու.	ուցումք-ուցուք-ուցո՛ւն.
4. Ուսան-իցիմ-իցիս-իցի.	իցիմք-իցիք-իցին.

INFINITIVE.

1. Շարժ-ել.
2. Լուան-ալ.
3. Հեղ-ուլ.
4. Ուսան-իլ or ել.

PARTICIPLE.

Present.

Հարժող or Հարժեցող. Լուացող. Հեղող. Ուսանող.

Past.

Հարժեալ. Լուացեալ. Հեղեալ. Ուսեալ.

Future.

Հարժելոց or Հարժելի. Լուանալոց or Լուանալի. Հեղլոց or Հեղլի. Ուսանելոց or Ուսանելի։

CONJUGATION OF SUBSTANTIVE VERBS

Defective verb Եմ, *I am.*

INDICATIVE.

Present.

Եմ, I am. ես, thou art. է, he is.
Եմք, we are. էք, ye are. են, they are.

Imperfect.

Էի, I was. էիր, thou wast. էր, he was.
Էաք, we were. էիք, ye were. էին, they were.

IMPERATIVE.

Ե՛ր, be thou *or* do thou be.
Է՛ք or երո՛ւք, be ye *or* do ye be.

SUBJUNCTIVE.

Իցեմ, I be. *իցես*, thou be. *իցէ*, he be.
Իցեմք, we be. *իցէք*, ye be. *իցեն*, they be.

INFINITIVE.

Ել, to be.

PARTICIPLE.

Past.

Եալ, been *or* having been.

Future.

Ելոց, which is to be, *or* about to be.

Comparing this verb with the verb *շարժել*, *to move*, of the first conjugation, it is clearly seen, that its conjugation is the basis of the latter.

Defective verb Գոմ, *I am* or *I exist.*

INDICATIVE.

Present.

Գոմ, I am. *գոս*, thou art. *գոյ*, he is.
Գոմք, we are. *գոյք*, ye are. *գոն*, they are.

Imperfect.

Գոյիր, thou wast. *գոյր*, he was.
Գոյին, they were.

SUBJUNCTIVE.

Future.

Գոլցէ, he be, it may be, it would be.
Գոլցեն, they be, they may be.

INFINITIVE.

Գոլ, to be, to exist.

PARTICIPLE.

Present.

Գոյող, being.

The deficiencies of this verb are supplied by the means of the other substantive verbs.

The word չիք is used sometimes as a substantive verb, as, *չիք իմ այր, I have no husband*, or *I am without a husband*, or *I am not married*. *ուսեալ բնաւ չիք, he has never learned.*

Substantive verb Եղանիմ, *I am made* or *done*.

INDICATIVE.

Present.

Եղանիմ, I am made. *եղանիս*, thou art made. *եղանի*, he is made.
Եղանիմք, we are made. *եղանիք*, ye are made. *եղանին*, they are made.

Imperfect.

Եղանէի, I was made. եղանէիր, thou wast made. եղանէր, he was made.
Եղանէաք, we were made. եղանէիք, ye were made. եղանէին, they were made.

Perfect.

Եղէ or եղայ, I have been. եղեր, thou hast been. եղեւ, he has been.
Եղաք or եղեաք, we have been. եղէք or եղայք, ye have been. եղեն, they have been.

Future.

Եղէց, I shall be. եղիցիս, thou shalt be. եղիցի, he shall be.

IMPERATIVE.

Present.

Մ՛ի եղանիր, be thou not. եղիցի՛, let him be.
Եղերո՛ւք, be ye. մի՛ եղանիք, be ye not. եղիցի՛ն, let them be.

SUBJUNCTIVE.

The present is formed like that of the Indicative.

Future.

Եղիցիմ or եղանիցիմ, I shall be made. եղիցիս, thou shalt be made. եղիցի, he shall be made.

Եղիցուք or եղանիցուք, we shall be made. եղիջիք, ye shall be made. եղիցին, they shall be made.

INFINITIVE.

Եղանիլ, to be, to be made, to be done.

PARTICIPLE.

Past.

Եղեալ, been, made, done, having been.

Future.

Եղանելոց or եղանելի, which is to be.

Substantive verb Լինեմ, *I am, I am made or done.*

INDICATIVE.

Present.

Լինիմ, I am. լինիս, thou art. լինի, he is. Լինիմք, we are. լինիք, ye are. լինին, they are.

Imperfect.

Լինէի, I was. լինէիր, thou wast. լինէր, he was.

Լինէաք, we were. լինէիք, ye were. լինէին, they were.

Future.

Լիցիմ, I shall be. լիցիս, thou shalt be. լիցի, he shall be.

Լիցուք, we shall be. լիցիք or լիջիք, ye shall be. լիցին, they shall be.

IMPERATIVE.

Present.

Լեր, be thou. մի՛ լինիր, be thou not. լիցի՛, let him be.

Լէ՛ք or լերո՛ւք, be ye. մի՛ լինիք, be ye not. լիցի՛ն, let them be.

Future.

Լիջի՛ր or լինիջի՛ր or լիցի՛ս, be thou. լիցի՛, let him be.

Լիցո՛ւք, let us be. լիջի՛ք or լինիջի՛ք, be ye. լիցի՛ն, let them be.

SUBJUNCTIVE.

Present is like that of the Indicative.

Future.

Լինիցիմ, I be *or* may be. լինիցիս, thou be. լինիցի, he be.

Լինիցիմք, we be. լինիցիք, ye be. լինիցին, they be.

INFINITIVE.

Լինել, to be.

PARTICIPLE.

Present.

Լինող, being.

Past.

Լեալ or լիեալ, been, having been.

Future.

Լինելոց or լինելի, which is to be.

FIRST CONJUGATION.

Active Շարժել, *To move.*

INDICATIVE.

Present.

Շարժեմ, I move. շարժես, thou movest. շարժէ, he moves.

Շարժեմք, we move. շարժէք, ye move. շարժեն, they move.

Imperfect.

Շարժէի, I moved *or* was moving. շարժէիր, thou movedst *or* wast moving. շարժէր, he moved *or* was moving.

Շարժէաք, we moved *or* were moving. շարժէիք, ye moved *or* were moving. շարժէին, they moved *or* were moving.

Perfect.

Շարժեցի, I moved. շարժեցեր, thou movedst. շարժեաց, he moved.

Շարժեցաք, we moved. շարժեցիք, ye moved. շարժեցին, they moved.

As we have remarked above, the Preterperfect, and Preter-plu-perfect are not properly formed in the Armenian language, because when the necessity occurs, they are accustomed to join the participle to the other tenses of the verb substantive.

Future.

Շարժեցից, I shall move. շարժեսցես, thou shalt move. շարժեսցէ, he shall move.

Շարժեսցուք, we shall move. շարժեսջիք, ye shall move. շարժեսցեն, they shall move.

IMPERATIVE.

Present.

Շարժեա՛, move thou. մի՛ շարժեր, move thou not. շարժեսցէ՛, let him move.

Շարժեցէ՛ք, move ye. մի՛ շարժէք, move ye not. շարժեսցե՛ն, let them move.

The negative particle մի՛, *not*, is also placed with the third person of the present, and before all the persons of the future in every conjugation.

Future.

Շարժեսջիր or շարժեսցես, move thou. շարժեսցէ, let him move.
Շարժեսցուք, let us move. շարժեսջիք, move ye. շարժեսցեն, let them move.

SUBJUNCTIVE.

The present is like that of the Indicative.

Future.

Շարժիցեմ, I move, I may, might, could, should, would move. շարժիցես, thou move, *etc.* շարժիցէ, he move, *etc.*
Շարժիցեմք, we move, *etc.* շարժիցէք, ye move, *etc.* շարժիցեն, they move, *etc.*

The future of the indicative, of the imperative, and of the subjunctive from their affinity are adopted by turns in all the four conjugations.

INFINITIVE.

Շարժել, to move.

PARTICIPLE.

Present.

Շարժող or շարժեցող, moving, who moves.

Past.

Շարժեալ or շարժեցեալ, having moved.

Future.

Շարժելոց, which has to move.

All the verbs active and neuter-active, which in the first person of the perfect end in եցի or ացի, are thus conjugated; and also the verbs Transitive ending in ուցի.

Passive Շարժիլ, *To be moved.*

The Passive of the first conjugation is formed by changing the ե in the last syllable of the Active into ի; the ցի into ցայ; the եց into այց: besides a few other variations.

INDICATIVE.

Present.

Շարժիմ, I am moved. շարժիս, thou art moved. շարժի, he is moved.
Շարժիմք, we are moved. շարժիք, ye are moved. շարժին, they are moved.

Imperfect.

Շարժէի, I was moved. շարժէիր, thou wast moved. շարժէր or շարժիւր; he was moved.
Շարժէաք, we were moved. շարժէիք, ye were moved. շարժէին, they were moved.

Perfect.

Շարժեցայ, I have been moved. շարժեցար, thou hast been moved. շարժեցաւ, he has been moved.

Շարժեցաք, we have been moved. շարժեցայք, ye have been moved. շարժեցան, they have been moved.

Future.

Շարժեցայց, I shall be moved. շարժեսցիս, thou shalt be moved. շարժեսցի, he shall be moved.

Շարժեսցուք, we shall be moved. շարժիջիք, ye shall be moved. շարժեսցին, they shall be moved.

IMPERATIVE.

Present.

Շարժեաց or շարժեցի՛ր, be thou moved. մի՛ շարժիր, be thou not moved. շարժեսցի՛, let him be moved.

Շարժեցարո՛ւք, be ye moved. մի՛ շարժիք, be ye not moved. շարժեսցի՛ն, let them be moved.

Future.

Շարժեսջի՛ր or շարժիջի՛ր, be thou moved. Շարժեսցի՛, let him be moved.

Շարժեսցո՛ւք, let us be moved. շարժիջի՛ք, be ye moved. շարժեսցի՛ն, let them be moved.

SUBJUNCTIVE.

Present is like that of the Indicative.

Future.

Շարժիցիմ, I shall be moved. շարժիցիս, thou shalt be moved. շարժիցի, he shall be moved.

Շարժիցիմք, we shall be moved. շարժիցիք, ye shall be moved. շարժիցին, they shall be moved.

INFINITIVE.

Շարժիլ or շարժել, to be moved.

PARTICIPLE.

Past.

Շարժեալ or շարժեցեալ, moved, being moved.

Future.

Շարժելոց or շարժելի, which is to be moved.

In this manner many Neuter-passive and Common verbs are conjugated.

Active Լուանալ, *To wash.*

INDICATIVE.

Present.

լուանամ, I wash. լուանաս, thou washest.
լուանայ, he washeth.
լուանամք, we wash. լուանայք, ye wash.
լուանան, they wash.

Imperfect.

լուանայի, I washed *or* was washing. լուանայիր, thou washedst *or* wast washing.
լուանայր, he washed *or* was washing.
լուանայաք, we washed *or* were washing.
լուանայիք, ye washed *or* were washing.
լուանային, they washed *or* were washing.

Perfect.

լուացի, I washed. լուացեր, thou washedst.
լուաց, he washed.
լուացաք, we washed. լուացիք, ye washed.
լուացին, they washed.

Future.

լուացից, I shall wash. լուասցես, thou shalt wash. լուասցէ, he shall wash.
լուասցուք, we shall wash. լուասջիք, ye shall wash. լուասցեն, they shall wash.

IMPERATIVE.

Present and *Future.*

Լուա՛, *լուասջի՛ր* or *լուացե՛ս*, wash thou. *մի՛ լուանար*, wash thou not. *լուասցէ՛*, let him wash.

Լ*ուասցո՛ւք*, let us wash. *լուացէ՛ք* or *լուասջի՛ք*, wash ye. *լուասցե՛ն*, let them wash.

SUBJUNCTIVE.

Future.

Լ*ուանայցեմ*, I wash, may wash, might wash, I could, should, would wash. *լուանայցես*, thou wash, *etc.* *լուանայցէ*, he wash, *etc.*

Լ*ուանայցեմք*, we wash. *լուանայցէք*, ye wash. *լուանայցեն*, they wash.

INFINITIVE.

Լ*ուանալ*, to wash.

PARTICIPLE.

Present.

Լ*ուացող*, washing, who washes.

Past.

Լ*ուացեալ*, having washed.

Future.

Լ*ուանալոց*, who has to wash.

Thus also are conjugated the verbs, which in the first person of the Perfect terminate in ցայ.

Passive Լուանել, *To be washed.*

INDICATIVE.

Present.

Լուանիմ, I am washed. լուանիս, thou art washed. լուանի, he is washed.
Լուանիմք, we are washed. լուանիք, ye are washed. լուանին, they are washed.

Perfect.

Լուացայ, I have been washed. լուացար, thou hast been washed. լուացաւ, he has been washed.
Լուացաք, we have been washed. լուացայք, ye have been washed. լուացան, they have been washed.

Future.

Լուացայց, I shall be washed. լուասցիս, thou shalt be washed. լուասցի, he shall be washed.
Լուասցուք, we shall be washed. լուասջիք, ye shall be washed. լուասցին, they shall be washed.

IMPERATIVE.

Present and *Future.*

Լուա՛, լուացի՛ր or լուասջի՛ր, be thou washed. լուասցի՛, let him be washed.

Լուասցուք, let us be washed. լուասջիք, be ye washed. լուասցին, let them be washed.

SUBJUNCTIVE.

Լուանայցիմ, I may be washed. լուանայցիս, thou mayst be washed. լուանայցի, he may be washed.

Լուանայցիմք, we may be washed. լուանայցիք, ye may be washed. լուանայցին, they may be washed.

INFINITIVE.

Լուանիլ, to be washed.

PARTICIPLE.

Past.

Լուացեալ, washed.

Future.

Լուանալի, which is to be washed.

The Passives of the second conjugation are not so harmonious to the ear, whence they are sometimes formed by means of the verbs substantive, or the actives are adopted with a passive sense.

THIRD CONJUGATION.

Active հեղուլ, *To pour out.*

INDICATIVE.

Present.

հեղում, I pour out. հեղուս, thou pourest out. հեղու, he pours out.
հեղումք, we pour out. հեղուք, ye pour out. հեղուն, they pour out.

Imperfect.

հեղուի, I poured out *or* was pouring out. հեղուիր, thou pour'dst out *or* wast pouring out. հեղոյր, he poured out *or* was pouring out.
հեղուաք, we poured out *or* were pouring out. հեղուիք, ye poured out *or* were pouring out. հեղուին, they poured out *or* were pouring out.

Perfect.

հեղի, I poured out. հեղեր, thou pour'dst out. եհեղ or հեղ, he poured out.
հեղաք, we poured out. հեղիք, ye poured out. հեղին, they poured out.

Future.

հեղից, I shall pour out. հեղցես, thou shalt pour out. հեղցէ, he shall pour out.

Հեղցուք, we shall pour out. *Հեղջիք*, ye shall pour out. *Հեղցեն*, they shall pour out.

IMPERATIVE.

Present and *Future.*

Հե՛ղ, *հեղջի՛ր* or *հեղցե՛ս*, do thou pour out. *Մի՛ հեղուր*, do thou not pour out. *Հեղցէ՛*, let him pour out.

Հեղցո՛ւք, let us pour out. *Հեղէ՛ք* or *հեղջի՛ք*, do ye pour out. *Մի՛ հեղուք*, do ye not pour out. *Հեղցե՛ն*, let them pour out.

SUBJUNCTIVE.

Future.

Հեղուցում, I pour out, I may, might, could, should, would pour out. *Հեղուցուս*, thou pour out, *etc*. *Հեղուցու*, he pour out, *etc*.

Հեղուցումք, we pour out, *etc*. *Հեղուցուք*, ye pour out. *Հեղուցուն*, they pour out.

INFINITIVE.

Հեղուլ, to pour out.

PARTICIPLE.

Present.

Հեղող, pouring out.

Past.

Հեղեալ, having poured out.

Future.

Հեղլոց, who has to pour out.

In this manner also are conjugated the verbs which in the first person of the Perfect terminate in այ or եայ.

Passive Հեղանել, *To be poured out.*

INDICATIVE.

Present.

Հեղանիմ, I am poured out. Հեղանիս, thou art poured out. Հեղանի, he is poured out.
Հեղանիմք, we are poured out. Հեղանիք, ye are poured out. Հեղանին, they are poured out.

Perfect.

Հեղայ, I have been poured out. Հեղար, thou hast been poured out. Հեղաւ, he has been poured out.
Հեղաք, we have been poured out. Հեղայք, ye have been poured out. Հեղան, they have been poured out.

Future.

Հեղայց, I shall be poured out. Հեղցիս, thou shalt be poured out. Հեղցի, he shall be poured out.
Հեղցուք, we shall be poured out. Հեղջիք, ye shall be poured out. Հեղցին, they shall be poured out.

IMPERATIVE.

հեղի՛ր or հեղցի՛ս, be thou poured out.
հեղցի՛, let him be poured out.
հեղարո՛ւք or հեղջի՛ք, be ye poured out.
հեղցի՛ն, let them be poured out.

INFINITIVE.

հեղանիլ, to be poured out.

PARTICIPLE.

Past.

հեղեալ, poured out.

Future.

հեղլի, which is to be poured out.

The deficiencies of the third conjugation passive are supplied from it's active.

FOURTH CONJUGATION.

Common verb Ուսանիլ, *To learn.*

INDICATIVE.

Present.

Ուսանիմ, I learn. ուսանիս, thou learnest.
ուսանի, he learns.
Ուսանիմք, we learn. ուսանիք, ye learn. ուսանին, they learn.

Imperfect.

Ուսանէի, I learned *or* was learning. ուսանէիր, thou learnedst *or* wast learning. ուսանէր, he learned *or* was learning.

Ուսանէաք, we learned *or* were learning. ուսանէիք, ye learned *or* were learning. ուսանէին, they learned *or* were learning.

Perfect.

Ուսայ, I have learned. ուսար, thou hast learned. ուսաւ, he has learned.

Ուսաք, we have learned. ուսայք, ye have learned. ուսան, they have learned.

Future.

Ուսայց, I shall learn. ուսցիս, thou shalt learn. ուսցի, he shall learn.

Ուսցուք, we shall learn. ուսջիք, ye shall learn. ուսցին, they shall learn.

IMPERATIVE.

Present.

Ուսի՛ր, learn thou. մի՛ ուսանիր, learn thou not. ուսցի՛, let him learn.

Ուսարո՛ւք, do ye learn. մի՛ ուսանիք, do ye not learn. ուսցի՛ն, let them learn.

Future.

Ուսջի՛ր or ուսանիջի՛ր, learn thou. ուսցի՛, let him learn.

Ուսցո՛ւք, let us learn. ուսջի՛ք or ուսանիջի՛ք, do ye learn. ուսցե՛ն, let them learn.

SUBJUNCTIVE.

The Present is like that of the Indicative.

Future.

Ուսանիցիմ, I learn, may, might, could, should, would learn. ուսանիցիս, thou learn, *etc.* ուսանիցի, he learn, *etc.*

Ուսանիցիմք, we learn. ուսանիցէք, ye learn. ուսանիցեն, they learn.

INFINITIVE.

Ուսանիլ or ուսանել, to learn.

PARTICIPLE.

Present.

Ուսանող, learning, who learns.

Past.

Ուսեալ, having learned.

Future.

Ուսանելոց or ուսանելի, who has to learn.

Thus are also conjugated the common verbs which in the first person of the Perfect terminate in ցայ.

They are at the same time active and passive.

Conjugations of the Irregular verbs.

ACTIVE.

INDICATIVE.

Present.

Առնեմ, I make. առնես, thou makest. առնէ, he makes.

Առնեմք, we make. առնէք, ye make. առնեն, they make.

Perfect.

Արարի, I have made. արարեր, thou hast made. արար, he has made.

INFINITIVE.

Առնել, to make, to do.

PARTICIPLE.

Present.

Արարող or առնող, making, who makes.

Past.

Արարեալ, having made, making.

Future.

Առնելոց, who has to make.

PASSIVE.

INDICATIVE.

Present.

Առնիմ, I am made. առնիս, thou art made. առնի, he is made.

Առնիմք, we are made. առնիք, ye are made. առնին, they are made.

Perfect.

Արարայ, I have been made. արարար, thou hast been made. արարաւ, he has been made.

Արարաք, we have been made. արարայք, ye have been made. արարան, they have been made.

INFINITIVE.

Առնիլ, to be made.

PARTICIPLE.

Past.

Արարեալ (not արարեցեալ) made.

Future.

Առնելի or առնելոց, which is to be made.

ACTIVE.

INDICATIVE.

Present.

Դնեմ, I put. դնես, thou putst. դնէ, he puts.
Դնեմք, we put. դնէք, ye put. դնեն, they put.

Perfect.

Եդի, I have put. եդիր or եդեր, thou hast put. եդ, he has put.
Եդաք, we have put. եդիք, ye have put. եդին, they have put.

INFINITIVE.

Դնել, to put, to place.

PARTICIPLE.

Present.

Դնող, putting.

Past.

Եդեալ, having put.

Future.

Դնելոց, who has to put.

PASSIVE.

INDICATIVE.

Present.

Դնիմ, I am put. դնիս, thou art put. դնի, he is put.

Դնիմք, we are put. դնիք, ye are put. դնին, they are put.

Perfect.

Եդայ, I have been put. եդար, thou hast been put. եդաւ, he has been put.
Եդաք, we have been put. եդայք, ye have been put. եդան, they have been put.

INFINITIVE.

Դնիլ, to be put.

PARTICIPLE.

Past.

Եդեալ (not դրեցեալ) put.

Future.

Դնելի or դնելոց, which is to be put.

ACTIVE.

INDICATIVE.

Present.

Լսեմ, I hear. լսես, thou hearest. լսէ, he hears.
Լսեմք, we hear. լսէք, ye hear. լսեն, they hear.

Perfect.

Լուայ, I heard. լուար, thou heard. լուաւ, he heard.

Լուաք, we heard. լուայք, ye heard. լուան, they heard.

INFINITIVE.

Լսել, to hear.

PARTICIPLE.

Present.

Լսող, hearing, who hears.

Past.

Լուեալ, having heared, hearing.

Future.

Լսելոց, who has to hear.

PASSIVE.

INDICATIVE.

Present.

Լսիմ, I am heard. լսիս, thou art heard. լսի, he *or* it is heard.

Լսիմք, we are heard. լսիք, ye are heard. լսին, they are heard.

Perfect.

Is formed by means of the Substantive verb, as,

Լուեալ, լսելի, լուր or լու եղէ, I have been heard. լուեալ եղեր, thou hast been heard. լուեալ եղեւ, he has been heard.

Լուեալ, լսելի, լուր or լու եղաք, we have been heard. լուեալ եղէք, ye have been heard. լուեալ եղեն, they have been heard.

INFINITIVE.

Լսիլ, to be heard.

PARTICIPLE.

Past.

Լուեալ, heard.

Future.

Լսելի, which is to be heard.
This verb is also regular.

ACTIVE.

INDICATIVE.

Present.

Ճանաչեմ, I know. ճանաչես, thou knowest. ճանաչէ, he knows.

Ճանաչեմք, we know. ճանաչէք, ye know. ճանաչեն, they know.

Perfect.

Ծանեայ, I have known. ծանեար, thou hast known. ծանեաւ, he has known.

Ծանեաք, we have known. ծանեայք, ye have known. ծանեան, they have known.

IMPERATIVE.

Ճանաչել, to know.

PARTICIPLE.

Present.

Ճանաչող, knowing, who knows.

Past.

Ծանուցեալ, having known.

Future.

Ճանաչելոց, who has to know.

PASSIVE.

INDICATIVE.

Present.

Ճանաչիմ, I am known. Ճանաչիս, thou art known. Ճանաչի, he is known.
Ճանաչիմք, we are known. Ճանաչիք, ye are known. Ճանաչին, they are known.

Perfect.

Ծանուցեալ եղէ, I have been known. Ծանուցեալ եղեր, thou hast been known. Ծանուցեալ եղեւ, he has been known.
Ծանուցեալ եղաք, we have been known. Ծանուցեալ եղէք, ye have been known. Ծանուցեալ եղեն, they have been known.

INFINITIVE.

Ճանաչիլ, to be known.

PARTICIPLE.

Past.

Ծանուցեալ, known.

This verb is also regular.

NEUTER

INDICATIVE.

Present.

Մեղանչեմ, I sin. մեղանչես, thou sinnest. մեղանչէ, he sins.

Մեղանչեմք, we sin. մեղանչէք, ye sin. մեղանչեն, they sin.

Perfect.

Մեղայ, I have sinned. մեղար, thou hast sinned. մեղաւ, he has sinned.

Մեղաք, we have sinned. մեղայք, ye have sinned. մեղան, they have sinned.

INFINITIVE.

Մեղանչել, to sin.

PARTICIPLE.

Present.

Մեղանչող, sinning, who sins.

Past.

Մեղուցեալ, having sinned.

Future.

Մեղանչելոց, who has to sin.
This verb is also regular.

NEUTER.

INDICATIVE.

Present.

Յառնեմ, I rise. յառնես, thou risest. յառնէ, he rises.
Յառնեմք, we rise. յառնէք, ye rise. յառնեն, they rise.

Perfect.

Յարեայ, I have been risen, I rose. յարեար, thou hast been risen. յարեաւ, he has been risen.
Յարեաք, we have been risen. յարեայք, ye have been risen. յարեան, they have been risen.

IMPERATIVE.

Արի, rise thou. մի յառներ, rise thou not.
Արիք, rise ye. մի յառնէք, rise ye not.

INFINITIVE.

Յառնել, to rise, to get up.

PARTICIPLE.

Past.

Յարուցեալ, risen, having been risen.

Future.

Յառնելոց, who is to rise.

ACTIVE.

INDICATIVE.

Present.

Տամ, I give. տաս, thou givest. տայ, he gives.
Տամք, we give. տայք, ye give. տան, they give.

Perfect.

Ետու, I have given. ետուր, thou hast given. ետ, he has given.
Տուաք, we have given. ետուք, ye have given. ետուն, they have given.

INFINITIVE.

Տալ, to give.

PARTICIPLE.

Present.

Տուող, giving, who gives.

Past.

Տուեալ, having given.

Future.

Տալոց, who has to give.

PASSIVE.

INDICATIVE.

Present.

Տուեալ լինիմ, I am given. տուեալ լինիս, thou art given. տուեալ լինի, he is given.
Տուեալ լինիմք, we are given. տուեալ լինիք, ye are given. տուեալ լինին, they are given.

Perfect.

Տուայ, I have been given. տուար, thou hast been given. տուաւ, he has been given.
Տուաք, we have been given. տուայք, ye have been given. տուան, they have been given.

INFINITIVE.

Տուեալ լինել, to be given.

PARTICIPLE.

Past.

Տուեալ, given.

Future.

Տալի, which is to be given.

NEUTER.

INDICATIVE.

Present.

Գամ, I come. գաս, thou comest. գայ, he cometh.
Գամք, we come. գայք, ye come. գան, they come.

Perfect.

Եկի, I was come. եկիր, thou wast come. եկն, he was come.
Եկաք, we were come. եկիք, ye were come. եկին, they were come.

INFINITIVE.

Գալ, to come.

PARTICIPLE.

Past.

Եկեալ, come, being come.

Future.

Գալոց, who is to come.

ACTIVE.

INDICATIVE.

Present.

Ուտեմ, I eat. ուտես, thou eatest. ուտէ, he eats.

Ուտեմք, we eat. ուտէք, ye eat. ուտեն, they eat.

Perfect.

Կերի or կերայ, I have eaten. կերեր or կերար, thou hast eaten. եկեր or կերաւ, he has eaten.

Կերաք, we have eaten. կերայք or կերիք, ye have eaten. կերին or կերան, they have eaten.

INFINITIVE.

Ուտել, to eat.

PARTICIPLE.

Present.

Կերող, eating, who eats.

Past.

Կերեալ, eating; having eaten.

Future.

Ուտելոց, who has to eat.

PASSIVE.

INDICATIVE.

Present.

Ուտիմ, I am eaten. ուտիս, thou art eaten. ուտի, he is eaten.

Ուտիմք, we are eaten. ուտիք, ye are eaten. ուտին, they are eaten.

Perfect.

Կերեալ եղէ, I have been eaten. կերեալ եղեր, thou hast been eaten. կերեալ եղև, he has been eaten.

Կերեալ եղաք, we have been eaten. կերեալ եղէք, ye have been eaten. կերեալ եղեն, they have been eaten.

INFINITIVE.

Ուտիլ, to be eaten.

PARTICIPLE.

Past.

Կերեալ, eaten.

Future.

Ուտելի or կերելի, which is to be eaten.

ACTIVE.

INDICATIVE.

Present.

Ըմպեմ, I drink. ըմպես, thou drinkest. ըմպէ, he drinks.

Ըմպեմք, we drink. ըմպէք, ye drink. ըմպեն, they drink.

Perfect.

Արբի, I drank. արբեր, thou drankest. արբ or էարբ, he drank.

Արբաք, we drank. արբէք, ye drank. արբին, they drank.

INFINITIVE.

Ըմպել, to drink.

PARTICIPLE.

Ըմպող, drinking, who drinks.

Past.

Ըմպեալ or Ըմբեալ, drunk *or* drunken; having drunk.

Future.

Ըմպելոց, who is to drink.

The passive is formed with a Substantive verb.

COMMON.

INDICATIVE.

Present.

Ունիմ, I take. ունիս, thou takest. ունի, he takes.

Ունիմք, we take. ունիք, ye take. ունին, they take.

Perfect.

Կալայ, I have taken. կալար, thou hast taken. կալաւ, he has taken.

Կալաք, we have taken. կալայք, ye have taken. կալան, they have taken.

INFINITIVE.

Առնել, to take, to have.

PARTICIPLE.

Present.

Առնող, taking, having, who has.

Past.

Կալեալ, taken, had; taking, having.

Future.

Առնելի or առնելոց, who has to take *or* to have.

NEUTER.

INDICATIVE.

Present.

Երթամ, I go. երթաս, thou goest. երթայ, he goes.

Երթամք, we go, երթայք, ye go. երթան, they go.

Perfect.

Չոգայ or չոգայ, I went *or* I am gone. չոգար, thou wentest *or* art gone. չոգաւ, he went *or* is gone.

Չոգաք, we went, *etc.* չոգայք, ye went. չոգան, they went *or* they are gone.

INFINITIVE.

Երթալ, to go.

PARTICIPLE.

Present.

Երթող, going, who goes.

Past.

Երթեալ, gone; going.

Future.

Երթալոց or երթալի, who is to go.

VERBS IMPERSONAL.

Those verbs are called Impersonal which are used only in the third person, as,

Ամպէ, it begins to cloud.
Անձրեւէ, it rains.
Ցօղէ, it rains little.
Հեղեղատէ, it comes pouring, it runs over.
Ձիւնէ, it snows.
Ճառագայթէ, it shines.
Առաւօտէ, it begins to be day-light.
Մրրկէ, it blows very hard.
Փայլատակէ, it lightens.
Պտղաբերէ, it produces fruit.
Մռնչէ, it bellows, it roars.
Կաղկանձէ, it howls.
Բառաչէ, it bellows, it roars.

Պարզանայ, it clears up.
Առաւօտանայ, it dawns.
Երեկոյանայ, it darkens.
Գիշերանայ, it is become night.
Լուսանայ, it brightens.
Խաւարանայ, it grows dusky.
Հրանայ, it kindles.
Որոտայ, it thunders.
Ասի, it is reported, they say.
Երևի, it appears, it seems.
Թուի, it seems.
Կարծի, 'tis believed, it is thought.
Լսի, it is noised abroad.
Հասանէ or հասանի, it happens, it falls out.
Պատահէ, it happens.
Հանդիպի, it happens.
Պիտի, it must, it behoves.
Ցաւէ or ցաւի, it pains.
Անկ է, it becomes, it is fit.
Արժան է, it is convenient, it becomes.
Անհնար է, it is impossible.
Բարւոք է, it is good, it is well.
Խիստ է, it is hard.
Կամ է or կամին են, it is wished, it wills.
Հարկ է, it must, it is necessary.
Մարթ է, it may be.
Յայտ է, it is clear.
Շատ է, it is enough, it sufficies.
Պարտ է, it must.
Վայել է, it is fit, it is proper.
Պէտք են, it must, it is necessary.
Օրէն է or օրէնք են, 'tis lawful, it allows.

Փոյթ է, it is cared for.
Օգուտ է, it is expedient.
Դէպ է, it is suitable, it is convenient, it becomes, it is fit.

PREPOSITION

A preposition is an indeclinable word or particle which placed before a noun changes either it's case, or it's signification.

The prepositions which change the cases of nouns are called *Formers of cases.*

The prepositions which change the meaning of nouns by governing their cases, are called *Rulers of cases.*

Prepositions ի, յ, ի յ and առ ի form the Dative and the Ablative.

Յ, ի յ are placed before the vowels.

Առ forms the Dative.

Ց forms the Dative. Before a consonant it is pronounced ըց, as, ըցնեղ.

Զ forms the Accusative. Before a consonant it was formerly pronounced զը, but at present it is pronounced ըզ.

Ընդ forms the Dative and the Ablative.

According to the modern usage the Prepositions forming the cases յ, ց and զ are written prefixed and joined to nouns, and the others detached from them.

A COLLECTION OF PREPOSITIONS.

Առ, առ'ի, *to, unto, towards, at: by, near, nigh: for, for the sake, on account: on, upon: under: against: amongst.* govern the dative, the genitive, and the instrumental cases.

Ընդ, *with: by: instead: for: under: between: to, unto, towards: on, upon: amongst.* governs the genitive, the dative, the ablative, and sometimes the instrumental.

Ըստ, *according: for: out, without: after.* governs the genitive, the dative, and the ablative.

Զերդ or զերթ, *as, like.* governs the accusative.

Իբր, իբրև or իբրու, *as, like, about.* govern generally the accusative.

Թարց or թանց, *without, out, unless.* governs the genitive.

Վասն, *for, in order to, concerning.* governs the genitive.

Քան, *than, much.* governs the accusative.

Ընթ see Ընդ.

Մինչ or մինչև, *till, untill, to, unto.* governs the dative with a preposition.

Հանդերձ, *with, by.* governs the instrumental.

Գեր, *over, above, upon, more, before, past.* governs generally the accusative, and sometimes the dative.

Պէս, *as, like.* governs the genitive and the dative.

Նման, նմանակ, *as, like.* governs the genitive and the dative.

Դէմ, *towards.* governs the dative.

Կոյս or կողմն, *towards.* govern the dative-with-preposition.

Մինչ, *till, untill, unto.* governs the instrumental.

Շուրջ, շուրջանակի, *about, around.* govern the circumdative.

Արտաքս, արտաքոյ, *out.* govern the genitive *or* the accusative with քան.

Փոխան, փոխանակ, *instead, inbehalf.* govern the genitive.

Ներքոյ or 'ի ներքոյ, *under.* govern the genitive.

'Ի վերայ, *on, upon.* governs the genitive.

'Ի վեր, վերոյ or 'ի վերոյ, *over, above.* govern the dative, *or* the accusative with քան.

'Ի մէջ or 'ի միջի, *in, into, in the middle, within, between, amongst.* govern the genitive.

'Ի միջոյ, *from the middle.* governs the genitive.

'Ի ձեռն, *by.* governs the genitive.

Օրէն, *as, like.* governs the genitive.

Զհետ, զհետի, զկնի, *after, behind.* govern the genitive.

Յաղագս or աղագաւ, *for, for the sake, because of.* govern the genitive.

'Ի *պատճառս* or *պատճառաւ*, *for, for the sake, because of.* govern the genitive.

'Ի *համար*, *on account, for.* governs the genitive.

Սակս or *'ի սակս*, *because of, for, on account.* govern the genitive.

'Ի *պէտս*, *for.* governs the genitive.

Յաջմէ or *ընդ աջմէ*, *on the right side.* govern the genitive.

'Ի *ձախմէ* or *ընդ ձախմէ*, *յահեկէ* or *ընդ ահեկէ*, *on the left side.* govern the genitive.

Բաց or *բայց*, *out, without, besides, except.* govern the ablative.

Զատ, *aside.* governs the ablative.

Հեռի, *far, far off.* governs the ablative.

Գաղտ, *secretly.* governs the ablative.

Ուրոյն, *apart, aside.* governs the ablative.

Քաւ, *God forbid.* governs the ablative.

Հուպ, *մերձ*, *մօտ*, *near, nigh, by.* govern the dative.

Կից, *conjoint, connected, with.* governs the dative.

Զոյգ, *joint, with.* governs the dative.

Նման, *like.* governs the dative.

Հակառակ, *against.* governs the dative.

Փոխարէն, *instead of.* governs the dative.

Առանց, *without, out, besides, unless.* governs the genitive.

Առաջի, *in front, before.* governs the genitive.

Յառաջոյ, *before, from before.* governs the genitive.

Ընդ առաջ, *against.* governs the genitive.

Ընթեր or առընթեր, *near, nigh, by.* govern the genitive and the dative.

Ընդդէմ, *against.* governs the genitive and the dative.

Դէմ ընդդէմ, դէմ յանդիման, հանդէպ, *in front, against, opposite.* govern the genitive and the dative.

Յանդիման, *before, in front.* governs the genitive and the dative.

Ակն յանդիման or յայտ յանդիման, *before, in front, evidently, publicly.* govern the genitive and the dative.

Մեկուսի, *apart, aside.* governs the ablative.

Յայսկոյս, *on this side.* governs the genitive.

Յայդ կոյս or յայնկոյս, *on that side, beyond, behind.* govern the genitive.

Յառաջ կոյս, *forwards.* governs the genitive.

Յետ կոյս, *back, backward, behind.* governs the genitive.

'Ի վեր կոյս, *onward.* governs the genitive.

'Ի վայր կոյս, *downward, downwards.* governs the genitive.

Դէպ վերոյ or գեր 'ի վերոյ, *above, higher, over than.* govern the dative and the ablative.

Որպէս, *as, like.* governs generally the accusative.

Վեր քան, 'ի վերոյ քան, գեր 'ի վերոյ քան, *above, higher, over than.* govern the accusative.

Առաւել քան, *over, above, more than*. governs the accusative.

Անդր քան, *beyond, further*. governs the accusative.

Յառաջ քան or նախ քան, *before, first than*. govern the accusative.

Արտաքոյ քան or արտաքս քան, *out than*. govern the accusative.

Յետոյ քան, *after than*. governs the accusative.

Some prepositions are rarely placed after the nouns.

ADVERB

An Adverb denotes the circumstances of a verb, or of an action.

A COLLECTION OF ADVERBS.

Այժմ, այժմու, արդ, ղարդիս, now, at present, actually, newly, recently.

Այժմէն, already, hence, from this time.

Այսօր or ՚ի ներկեանս, ՚ի ներկեան աւուր, to-day, in this day.

Վաղիւ, to-morrow.

Երեկ or յերեկն, yesterday.

Եռանդ or յեռանդն, the day before yesterday.

Ընդ երեկս, in the evening, towards the evening.

Գիշերի, գիշերայն or զգիշերայն, by night, in the night, in the night time.

Օմիջաւուրբ, at noon-day.

Վաղ քաջ, early, betimes.

Այգուն or այգուց, in the morning.

Վաղ ուրեմն, վաղու ևս, 'ի վաղուց, already.

Յայսմհետէ or յայսուհետև, henceforth, henceforward, hereafter.

Յորմէհետէ, since.

Յետոյ, զկնի, ապա, after, afterwards.

Երբեմն or մերթ, sometimes, now and then, from time to time.

Իբրև, երբ, յորժամ, մինչ, when, while, whilst.

Միշտ, յար, յարաժամ, հանապազ, ցանկ, յաւէժ, յաւէտ, always, ever, continually., every moment, evermore, for ever, eternally.

Դեռ, դեռևս, տակաւին, yet, still.

Մինչդեռ, այն մինչ, when, while, whilst, as long as.

Մինչև, till, untill.

Չև, չև ևս, մինչչև, not, not yet, not as yet.

Յայնժամ, then.

Ցայնժամ, till then.

Առժամայն, նոյնժամայն, նոյնհետայն; forthwith, very soon, in a moment, immediately, incontinently.

Յանկարծ, յանկարծուստ; յեղակարծ, suddenly, on a sudden, all of a sudden, unawares, in an unexpected manner.

Արագ, երագապէս, փոյթ, soon, as soon as, quickly, speedily, readily.

Ճեպով, շտապաւ, hastily, in haste.

Հուպ, հուպընդհուպ, presently, shortly, by and by, forthwith.

Հազիւ, հազիւ իմն, scarce, scarcely.

Իսկոյն, իսկ և իսկ, immediately, incontinently, forthwith, instantly.

Անագան, անագան ուրեմն, late, unseasonably.

Ուր ուրեմն, scarcely, rarely.

Տակաւ, տակաւ տակաւ, առ սակաւ սակաւ, by little and little, by degrees.

Աստ or *աստանօր*, here.

Աստէն, hence; here; in this world.

Աստի, աստուստ, hence, from hence.

Այր, here.

Այրէն, here, hitherward; by this way.

Այտի, thence, from thence.

Այդր, այդանօր, there.

Անդ, անդր, անդանօր or *անտանօր*, there.

Անդէն, thence, there: forthwith.

Անտի, անդուստ, thence, therefrom.

Անդստին, thence, from, since.

Յայս կոյս, on this side.

Յայնկոյս, on that side.

Արտաքս, 'ի դուրս, out, abroad.

'Ի ներքս, ներքոյ, within, inwardly.

Հեռի, 'ի բաց, 'ի բացեայ, far, afar, far off.

'Ի բացուստ, 'ի հեռաստանէ, from afar, from a great distance.

Մօտ, 'ի մօտոյ, near, nearly, at hand, closely.

Ստորև, 'ի ստորև, 'ի վայր, below, under, hereunder, beneath.

'Ի վեր, 'ի վեր անդր, up, upon, above, hereupon.

'Ի վերուստ, from above.

Ուր, ուրանօր, where.

Ուր ուրեք, where.

Ուստեք, from some place.

Ամենայն ուստեք, from every places.

Յառաջոյ, յառաջ կուսէ, from before.

Յետոյ, after, back, backward, behind.

Յետուստ, յետ կուսէ, 'ի թիկանց, from behind.

Յո՛, յոր կոյս, ընդ որ, where, which way.

Այլուր, somewhere else, elsewhere, in another place.

Այլուստ, from elsewhere, from another place.

Միանգամ, առ անգամ մի, առ մի նուագ, once, at one time.

Երկիցս, twice.

Երիցս, thrice.

Չորիցս, four times over.

Հնգիցս, five times over.

Վեցիցս, six times over.

Նախ, նախ առաջին, զառաջինն, first, at first, the first time, in the first place, at the beginning, before.

Երկրորդ, ապա, secondly, after, then.

Մի—միւս, one—another, first—in the second place.

Քանիցս, քանիցս անգամ, how often, how much time, how many times.

Բազում անգամ, յոլովակի, յաճախակի, յոքնակի, oft, often, mostly, many *or* several times, frequently.

Մի ըստ միոջէ, one after another, orderly.

Մի քան զմի, one more than another.

Փոխանակաւ, փոփոխ, by turns, reciprocally, interchangeably, mutually.

Յետ զհետէ, successively, one after another.

Կրկին, կրկնակի, doubly, twice.

Դարձեալ, վերստին, միւսանգամ, անդրէն, again, moreover, once more.

'Ի վերջէ or 'ի վերջոյ, last, lastly, at last.

Է՞ր, զի՞, զմէ՞, հի՞մ, առ ի՞մէ, ընդէ՞ր, է՞ր վասն, վասն է՞ր, յո՞յր սակս, է՞ր ո՞ւմ, առ ի՞նչ, why? wherefore? for why? for what reason?

Զի՞նչ, what? which?

Զիա՞րդ, ի՞բր, ո՞րպէս, how? in what manner? why?

Ո՞չ, ո՞չ ապաքէն, is it not?

Քանի՞ոն, how much?

Ի՞ւ, ի՞ւ իւիք, by which? how?

Մի՞, մի՞թէ — եթէ, or — either?

Ո՞ւստ, from whence?

Ե՞րբ, յո՞րժամ, when?

Այո՛, yes.

Արդարեւ, յիրաւի, հաւաստեաւ, իսկապէս,

անշուշտ, truly, verily, certainly, surely, indeed, in truth, assuredly, infallibly, undoubtedly, justly, really.

Կարի՛ քաջ, very well.

Ապաքէն, արդեօք, truly, verily.

Գրեթէ, գո՛գ, գոգցես, almost, nearly, as it were, pretty near.

Ո՛ն և ո՛ն, so, thus.

Գուցէ, գուցէ թէ, գուցէ երբեք, թերևս, արդեօք, իցէ թէ, իցէ զի, perhaps, lest, it may be.

Միթէ, մի՛ արդեօք, may it be.

Չ, ո՛չ, no, not.

Եւ ո՛չ, nor, neither.

Ո՛չ ևս, no more.

Ո՛չ բնաւ, ամենևին ո՛չ, never, by no means.

Ոչ ինչ, nothing.

Այլ ո՛չ ևս, no more.

Մի՛, մի՛ բնաւ, մի՛ երբեք, մի՛ լիցի, մի՛ իւիք, no, not, never, by no means.

Ո՛ն անդր, forbear.

Քա՛ւ, God forbid, forbear.

Միայն, եւեթ, լոկ, սոսկ, only, but.

Միայնակ, միայն ընդ միայն, singly, solely.

Մի մի, one by one.

Մեկուսի, ուրոյն, առանձինն, առանձնակի, apart, aside, asunder, separately, singly, particularly.

Ահա՛, behold, lo, see, there.

Ահաւասիկ or *աւասիկ*, behold, here.

Ահաւադիկ or *աւադիկ*, behold, there.

Ահաւանիկ or *աւանիկ*, there, behold.

Նա՛, մանաւանդ, նա՛ մանաւանդ, այն զի, յաւէտ, առաւել, առ՛, առ՛նա, rather, more, than, nay, chiefly.
Ինձէն, by my-self.
Քեզէն, by thy-self.
Մեզէն, by our-selves.
Ձեզէն, by your-selves.
Այժմէն, from since, from this time.
Ինքնին, by himself.
Գլխովին, almost, quite, totally.
Բոլորովին or բոլորովինք, wholly, totally, entirely.
Կամաւ or կամովին, voluntarily, willingly.
Երբեք, ever, at any time.
Ուրեք, in some place.
Ուստի, whence, from whence.
Կարի, too, much, most, too much.
Իւրովի, by himself.
Ձրի, freely, for nothing, gratis.
Ուժգնակի, violently, vehemently.
Կողմնակի, side-ways, obliquely.
Ուղղակի, directly, perpendicularly, in a straight line.
Ձեռամբացի, with *or* by hand.
Նշանացի, with a sign.
Աքացի, by *or* with kicking.
Հայերէն or Հայեցի, in Armenian.
Եբրայեցերէն, in Hebrew.
Հրէարէն, in the Jewish language.
Յունարէն, in Greek.
Կենդանւոյն, alive.
Ազգովինք, nationally, with whole family.

Ամենեւիմբ, wholly, totally.
Դիւրաւ or հեշտեաւ, easily, readily, without trouble, at leisure.
Ընաւ, totally, almost, ever.
Խստիւ, severely, cruelly, rudely, hardly.
Կանխաւ, before, beforetime, formerly.
Ճշդիւ, exactly; sparingly.
Ճշմարտիւ, truly, indeed, really, certainly.
Մեղմով, softly, gently, slowly, mildly, quietly, peaceably.
Բարւոք or բարւոքապէս, well, rightly.
Ի բնէ, naturally, by nature, radically, originally.
Յառաջնմէ or յառաջուց, before, already; primitively, formerly.
Ի մասնէ, partly, in part.
Յոյժ, too, much, too much, very much, most.
Յարժանի, worthily, justly.
Առաւօտու or առաւօտուց, in the morning.
Յանչափս, exceedingly, excessively, immoderately, extremely.
Մարդկօրէն, մարդկաբար, մարդկապէս, humanly, as a man.
Արտաքուստ, from without, outwardly.
Յայնմհետէ, thenceforth, thenceforward.
Նոյնչափ, so much, so many.
Միանգամայն, at once, together.
Ի հարեւանցի, superficially, carelessly.
Արագ արագ, fast, hastily, quickly, speedily, soon.

Որպէս, as, how.
Որչափ, որքան, որգոն, as.
Համօրէն, totally, wholly, altogether.
Ընդ վայր, in vain, needless, to no purpose.
Այլընդայլոյ, diversly, otherwise, contrarily.
Ընդ ամենայն, altogether, totally, wholly.
Եւս քան զեւս, more and more.
Այսպէս, սոյնպէս, so, in this manner.
Այդպէս, դոյնպէս, so, thus, in that manner.
Այնպէս, նոյնպէս, thus, in that manner.
Նմանապէս, in like manner, so, thus.
Նոյնօրինակ, alike, so, thus.
Միօրինակ, alike, equally, in the same manner.
Զիարդ, որպէս զիարդ, as, like, how.
Զորօրինակ, as, for example.
Չարաչար, badly, sadly, ill, miserably, cruelly.
Այլապէս, այլազգաբար, diversly, otherwise.
Յայտնի, յայտնապէս, evidently, clearly, openly, publicly.
Մեկին, մեկնօրէն, explicitly, plainly, openly, clearly.
Լու 'ի լու, publicly, openly.
Ծածուկ, 'ի ծածուկ, ծածկաբար, գաղտնաբար, secretly, in secret, under hand.
Լռելեայն, լռիկ իմն, silently, tacitly, quietly.
Դիւրաբար, easily.
Բռնի, բռնաբար, forcibly, by force, violently.

Դժուարաւ, hardly, not easily, scarcely.

'Ի հարկէ, հարկաւ, necessarily, inevitably.

Յակամայս, unwillingly, forcibly, with regret.

Կամակար, 'ի կամակարուց, willingly, voluntarily, readily.

Զուր, 'ի զուր, տարապարտուց, վայրապար, ընդ վայր, 'ի նանիր, in vain, vainly, to no purpose, without any reason.

Յանդէպս, unfitly, improperly, amiss, absurdly.

Յանգէտս, ignorantly, unknowingly.

Նենգաւ, by fraud, fraudulently, deceitfully.

'Ի մերկուց, nakedly.

Հետի, հետիոտս, on foot.

Նորոգ, newly, recently, freshly, lately, just now.

Այսչափ, այսքան, so much, so many.

Այդչափ, այդքան, so much, so many.

Որչափ, որքան, as much, how much, how many, as far.

Համանգամայն, միանգամայն, 'ի միասին, առ հասարակ, together, altogether, all at once, wholly, totally, completely, entirely, in the mean while.

Շատ, much, many, greatly, a great deal, very, enough.

Յաւէտ, առաւել, more, at most, too much, very much.

Առաւել ևս, more than.

Սակաւ, սակաւ մի, սակաւիկ ինչ, խուն մի, խուն ինչ, փոքր մի, դոյզն ինչ, փոքր 'ի շատէ, little, but little, some, somewhat, something, less, in a small quantity.

Բաւականապէս, sufficiently, well enough, duly, tolerably.

CONJUNCTION

A Conjunction is an indeclinable word which connects the parts of speech together, or one sense with another.

A COLLECTION OF CONJUNCTIONS.

Եւ, և or ու, and, or.

Եւս, ևս և, և ևս, այլ, այլև, նաև, նաևս, իսկ, դարձեալ, also, too, still, yet, more, even.

Կամ, և կամ, կամ թէ, թէ, եթէ, or, either.

Բայց, բայց, սակայն, համայն, այլ սակայն, բայց սակայն, բայց միայն, բայց եթէ, միայն, միայն թէ, քան թէ, եթէ ոչ, but, only, unless, except, save, nevertheless, notwithstanding, however, yet, provided, upon condition that, if not.

Թէ և, թէպէտ, թէպէտև, though, although, however.

Թէ և ո՛չ, though not.

Ո՛չ եթէ, իբր ո՛չ եթէ, no, not.

Ո՛չ միայն, not only.

Ա՛յս է, այն է, նա է, այսինքն, այսինքն է, it is, that is to say, to wit.

Որպէս, իբր, իբրև թէ, որպէս այն թէ, իբր այն թէ, as, if it were.

Ըստ որում, as, how.

Օրինակ իմն, զորօրինակ, as, for example.

Ա.րդ, և արդ, այլ արդ, բայց արդ, իսկ արդ, ապաքէն, then, therefore, in consequence, now.

Ա.յն զի, rather.

Զի, քանզի, վասն զի, որպէս զի, փոխանակ զի, այնու զի, այն զի, նա զի, որովհետև, մինչ, for, because, that, whereas, forasmuchas, in order to, to the end that, since.

Ուր, where.

Որ, that.

Ապա, ուրեմն, ապաքէն, ապա ուրեմն, նա ուրեմն, ուստի, վասն որոյ, այսր աղագաւ, սմին իրի, դմին իրի, նմին իրի, այսուհետև, then, therefore, wherefore, in *or* by consequence, for this reason.

Քան, քան թէ, առաւել, մանաւանդ, յաւէտ, նա, թող թէ, than, rather, at most, on the contrary.

Մինչ, մինչև, մինչզի, անդամ, զի, զի և, so that, till, untill.

Թէ, եթէ, իսկ թէ, ապա թէ, ապա եթէ or ապեթէ, if.

Ապա թէ ոչ, otherwise.

Գէթ, գոնէ, գոնեայ, at least.

Թէ, եթէ, և թէ, զի, բայ, բամ, որ, that.

INTERJECTION

An Interjection expresses the passions of the soul.

A COLLECTION OF INTERJECTIONS.

Երանի, երանի թէ, յանկարծ, եղէ թէ, եղիցի, ով, օչ, would to God, may it be!

Ո՜, ո՜վ, ո՜վ թէ, բա՜բէ, վա՜շ, oh! oh! wonderful! see! o God!

Ո՛ ո, ով, ոհ, ոհ ոհ, էհ, ըհ, վայ, վայ վայ, ա՛ ա, ափսոս, աղէտ, աւաղ, եղուկ, բաբէ, oh! alas! woe be to! poor! wretch that!

Վաշ, վաշ վաշ, ոհ ոհ, oh joy!

Վա՜հ, վա՜շ, ո՜հ, յէ՜հ, է՜հէ, հը՜ հը, ա՜յ, է՜, a! ah!

Ա՜յ, ով, ճշտ, պյմ, o! fie! pish!

Ա՜ղէ, հա՜պա, օ՜ն, հա՜, come, come on, cheer, well well.

Թո՛ղ, forbear.

Ա՛ծ, բեր, bring, come.

Ե՛կ, եկ բեր, come, come bring.

SYNTAX

Syntax is the due conjunction or connexion of the parts of speech.

Substantives agree with each other in three ways.

1. When another substantive is added to express and explain the former more fully, as, Կղէոպատրաւ դստերբն համդերձ. with *Cleopatra* his *daughter*. Ետ զԿղէոպատրա դստր իւր. he has given *Cleopatra* his *daughter*. Տեսանել զեղբարսն իւրովք, զորդիսն Իսրայելի. to visit his *brethren the children* of Israel.

2. When one thing is said to belong to another, as, Գիրք ծննդեան Յիսուսի Քրիստոսի՝ որդւոյ Դաւթի՝ որդւոյ Աբրահամու. the book *of the generation of Jesus* Christ, the son *of David*, the son *of Abraam*. Տային վկայութիւն առաքեալքն յարութեանն Տեառն. gave the apostles witness *of the resurrection of the Lord*.

3. When a substantive or gerund like a verb governs another substantive, as, Յետ ընդունելութեան գիտութեան ճշմարտութեանն. after that *we have received the knowledge* of the truth. Ապստամբութեան ուսուցանես ՚ի Մովսէսէ՝ որոց ՚ի հեթանոսս ամենայն Հրէայք են. thou teachest all the Jews which are among the Gentiles *to forsake Moses*. Բայց զհոգւոյն հայհոյութեան մի թողցի. but the

blasphemy against the (Holy) Ghost shall not be ſorgiven .

Substantives agree with Adjectives when governed by the same, as, Մ՛եզ մատակարարք լինէին նոցին՝ որք այժմ պատմեցան . unto us *they did minister the things*, which are now reported. Ծնողս անարգողք . disobedient to parents. Եղէգն շարժուն 'ի հողմոյ . a reed *shaken with the wind.* Գեղեցիկ 'ի տեսա- նել, և քաղցր 'ի կերակուր . that is pleasant to the sight, and good for food. Եւ 'ի կա- նանց գլխաւորաց ոչ սակաւք . and *of the* chief *women* not *a few.* Ետես կոյր մի 'ի ծնէ . he saw a man which was *blind from* his *birth* . Եւ Աբրամ էր մեծատուն յոյժ անասնովք, և արծաթով, և ոսկւով . and Abram was very *rich in cattle, in silver*, and *in gold.* Բայց Ռաքէլ եարն էր տեսլեամբ , և գեղեցիկ երեսօք . but Rachel was *beautiful* and *well-favored* . Ողջամիտս 'ի հաւատս, 'ի սէր, 'ի համբե- րութեան . sound in faith, in charity, in pa- tience. Եւ մեծն 'ի ձէնջ՝ եղիցի ձեր սպասա- ւոր . but he that is *greatest among you* shall be your servant . Կրտսերագոյն յորդւոց նորա . *the youngest of* his *sons.*

The Comparatives govern generally the Accusative with the preposition քան, as, Զի կարի զօրաւորագոյն քան զմեզ եղեր . for thou art much *mightier than we.* Մ՛եծ քան զՅով- նան է աստ . *a greater than Jonas* is here.

Also the Middle nouns govern different

cases, as, Ահա Ադամ եղեւ իբրեւ զմի 'ի մէնջ. behold, the man (Adam) is become as *one of us*. Ո՞վ սրբեսցէ զանձն իւր 'ի կանանցածնաց. *how* can *he* be clean *that is born of a woman?* Եւ ոչ հեռի իսկ է յիւրաքանչիւր ումեքէ 'ի մէնջ. though he be not far *from every one of us*. Զայլ ոք յԱռաքելոց անտի ոչ տեսի. but *other of the Apostles* saw I none.

CONCORDANCE OF ADJECTIVES WITH SUBSTANTIVES.

1. The adjective may be placed before or after the substantive; joined, or divided from it.

2. The adjective may or may not be of the same case or number with the substantive.

3. The governing preposition may be placed either before the substantive or adjective, or before both being repeated.

Examples.

Կենդանի եւ մշտնջենաւոր բանիւն Աստուծոյ. *by the word* of God, *which liveth* and *abideth of ever*. Մեծաւն եւ կատարելովն եւ անձեռագործ խորանաւն. *by a greater* and *more perfect tabernacle*, not made with hands. 'Ի վերայ մերկոյ պարանոցի նորա. upon *the smooth of* his *neck*. Եփեսցես զմիս նորա 'ի սրբում տեղւոջ. seethe his flesh *in the holy place*. Վասն ամենայն եղելոց զօրութեանցն. for all *the migh-*

ty works. Դարձան յԵրուսաղէմ յանուանեալ լեռնէն Ձիթենեաց. returned they unto Jerusalem *from the mount called* Olivet. Եւ մեծամեծս և ս քան զսոյնս ցուցանէ նմա գործս. and he will shew him *greater works* than these. Եւ պատժեաց Աստուած զՓարաւոնն պատժօք մեծամեծօք և չարօք և զտուն նորա. and the Lord plagued Pharaoh and his house *with great plagues*. Կէսն քեղկէն աւելորդա մնայելով ծածկեսցէ զապարանս փեղկից խորանին յետոյ կողմանէ. *the half-curtain that remaineth*, shall hang over the backside of the tabernacle. Որք և լսիցեն զանուանէ քումդ մեծէ, և զզօրանէ քումդ հզօրէ, և զբազկէ քումդ ձգելոյ. for they shall hear *of thy great name*, and *of thy strong hand*, and *of thy stretched-out arm*. Եկն կին մի որ ունէր շիշ եղելոյ նարդեան՝ ազնուի մեծագնոյ. there came a woman having an alabaster-box *of ointment of spikenard, very precious*. Տեսի զՏէր նստեալ յաթոռ բարձրութեան և վերացելոյ. I saw also the Lord sitting *upon a throne*, high and *lifted up*. Տէր, զազգ մի զանգէտ և զարդար կորուսանիցես. Lord, wilt thou slay also a *righteous nation*? Ի մարդոյ մեղաւորէ նենգաւորէ փրկեա զիս. o deliver me *from the deceitful and unjust man*. Բայց զլեզու մարդկան ոչ ոք կարէ հնազանդել՝ զչարն և զանկարգ և լի թունովք մահաբերիւն. but *the tongue* can no man tame: *it is an unruly evil, full* of deadly poison. Յուսմունս պէսպէսս և յօտարաձայնս. with divers and strange doctrines. *Որ հարցն եղելոյ աւե-տեացն.* *of the promise made* unto our fathers. *'Ի բերանոյ երկուց և երից վկայից հաստատես-ցի ամենայն բան.* in the mouth *of two* or *three witnesses* every word may be established. *Նոյ էր ամաց վեցհարիւրոց.* Noah was *six hundred years* old. *Իբրև ասպարիսօք հնգետա-սանս.* about *fifteen furlongs* off. *'Ի վեցհա-րիւրորդի և 'ի միում ամի յամսեանն առաջ-նում.* in the six hundredth and first year, in the first month. *Այնչափ գնոյ զգեօղն վա-ճառեցիք. և նա ասէ, այո՛ այնչափ.* whether ye sold the land *for so much?* and she said, yea, *for so much.* *Այս այնպիսի.* such a one as this is. *Զի զօրութիւնք այսպիսիք 'ի ձեռաց սորա լինիցին.* that even *such mighty works* are wrought by his hands. *Յորմէ՞ աշ-խարհէ ես, կամ յորմէ՞ ժողովրդենէ.* *what* is *thy country?* and *of what people* art thou? *Որով դատաստանաւ դատիք.* *with what judgement* ye judge. *Զի՞նչ վնաս է իմ, կամ զի՞նչ յանցանք են իմ.* *what* is my *trespass*, *what* is my *sin?* *Հանդերձ ծերովք ոմամբք, և ճարտա-րախօսաւ Տերտիւղեաւ ումամբ.* with *the elders*, and with *a certain orator* named *Tertulus.* *Եգիտ հրեայ ոմն անուն Ակիւղաս.* and found *a certain Jew* named Aquila. *'Ի հո-վուէ միոջէ.* from one shepherd. *Զբան ինչ մեծ առ քեզ հասուցանիցեն, և զփոքր ինչ դա-տաստան ինքեանք դատեսցեն.* *Every great matter* they shall bring unto thee: but *every small matter* they shall judge. *Նա՝ աւանիկ*

ԱՌԼԱՒԱԳՈՅՆ ԻՆՉ *ցանկացեալ են, այս ինքն է՝* ԵՐԿՆԱՒՈՐԻՆ. but now they desire *a better* country, that is, *an heavenly*. *Առանց իրիք խղճելոյ*. doubting nothing. ՚Ի *գալ* ՄԻՒՍՈՅ *շաբաթուն*. *the next sabbath* (or sabbath-day.) *Այլովք բանիւք բազմօք*. with many other words. *Առ այլ երինջովք*. by the other kine. ՚Ի *դառնալ ձեզ* ԻՒՐԱՔԱՆՉԻՒՐ *՚ի չարեաց ձերոց*. in turning away *every one of you* from his iniquities. ՚Ի *վերայ միոյ ուրուք ՚ի լերանց*. upon some mountain.

Notwithstanding the great licence in the use of adjectives the following rules must be generally observed.

1. The adjective placed after the substantive must agree with it in number and case, as, *քարամբք մեծամեծօք, with great stones. զօրութիւնք այսպիսիք, such mighty works*.

2. The adjective placed before a substantive does not agree with it, excepting the monosyllable adjectives, as, *մեծամեծ քարամբք, with great stones. այսպիսի զօրութիւնք, such mighty works. այլովք բանիւք, with other words. ՚ի սրբում տեղւոջ, in the holy place.*

3. When a verb or participle is before the substantive and after the adjective, the adjective agrees readily with the substantive, as, *աստուածայնով զինէ զօրութեամբ, he armeth with divine force. աստուածայնով զի-*

նեալ զօրութեամբ, armed with divine force.

4. An adjective with the article or the letter distinctive of the person, placed before a substantive, agrees with it in number and in case, but not always, as, *մեծաւն և կատարելովն և անձեռագործ խորանաւն, by a greater and more perfect tabernacle, not made with hands.*

5. When there are many substantives before one adjective only, the adjective is in the plural, and agrees with them, as, *Սաւուղ և Յովնաթան սիրելիք և գեղեցիկք և վայելուչք, Saul and Jonathan* (were) *lovely and pleasant.*

6. The governing preposition is joined to the case which precedes it, whether substantive or adjective, as, *յանուանեալ լեռնէն, from the mount called. 'ի մարդոյ մեղաւորէ նենգաւորէ, from the deceitful and unjust man.*

7. When the adjectives or substantives placed before are joined with the conjunction *և*, *and*, the governing preposition is applied to all, as, *յանեղծ և յանարատ և յանթառամ ժառանգութիւնն, to an inheritance incorruptible, and undefiled, and that fadeth not away. 'ի հնազանդութիւն և 'ի հեղումն արեանն, unto obedience and sprinkling of the blood.*

8. When the adjective or substantive placed before is simple, and many substantives or adjectives follow, the governing pre-

position governs the first word, and the second and third which follow; however not always, as, *'ի չար խորհրդոց, 'ի բանից և 'ի գործոց, from evil thoughts, words, and works. զայր արիւնահեղ և զնենգաւոր, the bloody and deceitful man.*

CONCORDANCE OF PRONOUNS.

The personal pronouns *ես, I, դու, thou, ինքն, he* or *himself*, are substantives, and as substantives agree with adjectives, as, *Վասն ձեր կեղծաւորաց, of you hypocrites.*

Ինքն signifies sometimes *self*, as, *Ես ինքն մարդ եմ. I myself also am a man.*

The definitive pronouns *սա, դա, նա, he* (*she, it*) are substantives, and so agree with adjectives, as, *Դոքա յետինքդ. these last. Եւ կամ ինքեանք սոքա ասասցեն. or else let these same here say.*

The definitive pronouns *սոյն, դոյն, նոյն, this, that, same*, are adjectives, and so agree with substantives, as, *'Ի սոյն* or *'ի սմին աւուր. on this day*, or *in the course of this day*, or *to day. Ըստ դմին օրինակի. in the like manner. 'Ի նմին զանգուածոյ. of the same lump. Յորոգայթ 'ի նոյն անկցի. into that very destruction let him fall. Եւ սմին այսմիկ զամենայն փոյթ 'ի մէջ առեալ. and besides this, giving all diligence.*

The definitive pronouns *այս, this, այդ, այն, that*, are generally adjectives, but sometimes substantives, as, Զի՞նչ գործեցեր զայդ. *what is this that thou hast done?* Այս են ծնունդք որդւոցն ՝Նոյի. *these are the generations of the sons of Noah.* Յայս երկուս պատուիրանս. *on these two commandments:* Որոց զայս ընդ միմեանս երդմունս արարեալ էր. *who had made this conspiracy.* Եթէ եղեա՞լ իցէ ըստ բանիս մեծի այսորիկ. *whether there hath been any such thing as this great thing is?* ՝Ի չարեացդ քոց յայդցանէ. *of this thy wickedness.* Թղթովդ այդուիկ. *by this epistle.* Ըստ ամենայն բանիցս այսոցիկ, և ըստ ամենայն տեսլեանս այսորիկ. *according to all these words, and according to all this vision.* Երանի որ պահէ զբանս մարգարէութեանս զայս. *blessed is he that keepeth the sayings of the prophecy.* Յազգէ յայդմանէ. *of this generation.* Անձինք ծառայից քոց այսոցիկ յիսնից. *the life of these fifty thy servants.* Կեցցե՞մ ՝ի հիւանդութենէ աստի իմմէ յայսմանէ. *shall I recover of this disease?* Զայն Մովսէս՝ զոր ուրացանն ... զնա Աստուած իշխան և փրկիչ առաքեաց. *this Moses, whom they refused ... the same did God send to be a ruler and a deliverer.*

The possessive pronouns իմ, *my*, քո, *thy*, մեր, *our*, ձեր, *your*, իւր, *his*, *his own*, are adjectives. When they are without substantives, receive either the articles ս, դ, ն, or the adverbs աստէ, անտէ, as, ՝Քո՛ է ամենայն ինչ, և ՝ի քոյոցդ տուաք քեզ. *all things come of thee, and thine own have we given thee.* Հանգեաւ յիւրոց գործոց անտի, որպէս և Աստուած յիւրայոցն. *he also hath ceased from his own works, as God did from his.*

The pronouns possessive derived իմային or իմոյին, *my*, ձերային or ձերոյին, *your's*, are put before the substantives.

The pronoun relative որ, *who*, *which*, *what*, *that*, is substantive, and in different manners agrees with antecedent and following nouns, as, Աչս՝ որովք ոչ տեսանիցեն, և ականջս՝ որովք ոչ լսիցեն, *Eyes that they should not see, and ears that they should not hear.* Լուաւ 'ի նմանէ վասն որ 'ի Քրիստոս Յիսուս հաւատոցն, *heard him concerning the faith in Christ.* Զի մի ինչ եկեսցէ 'ի վերայ իմ յորոց դուքդ ասէք, *that none of these things which ye have spoken come upon me.* Որում խնդրէ 'ի քէն՝ տուր, և որ կամի փոխ առնուլ 'ի քէն՝ մի դարձուցաներ զերեսս, *give to him that asketh thee, and from him that would borrow of thee turn not thou away.* 'Ի վախճան աւուրցս այսոցիկ խօսեցաւ ընդ մեզ որդւովն, զոր եդ ժառանգ ամենայնի, որով և զյաւիտեանսն արար, որ է լոյս փառաց, *hath in these last days spoken unto us by his son, whom he hath appointed heir of all things, by whom also he made the worlds. Who being the brightness of his glory.* Եւ պատմեաց Մովսէս Ահարոնի զամենայն պատգամսն՝ զոր առաքեաց զնա Տէր, *and Moses told Aaron all the words of the*

Lord who had sent him. Եւ ամենայն արք տան նորա՝ ընտանիք և արծաթագնիք՝ որ էին յազգաց օտարաց, թլփատեաց զնոսա, *and all the men of his house, born in the house, and bought with money of the stranger, were circumcised with him.* Յորոց դուն 'ի խնդիր երթեալ էիր, *which thou wentest to seek.* Որոց զարիւնն Պիղատոս խառնեաց ընդ զոհսն նոցա, *whose blood Pilate had mingled with their sacrifices.* Առ որ մատուցեալ 'ի վէմն կենդանի, *to whom coming, as unto a living stone.* Որոյ սերմն իւր 'ի նմին, *whose seed is in itself.* Եւ ժողովեցին, որ շատ, և որ սակաւ, *and gathered, some more, some less.*

The articles-distinctive-of the persons ս of the first, դ of the second, ն of the third, besides showing the persons joined to the terminations of words, have also the force of the English articles *a* and *the*, and give energy and ornament, as, Տէր և Վարդապետ (without any article) *Lord and Master,* but with the article ս so, Տէրս և Վարդապետս, it may have three senses: 1°. *I who am a Lord and a Master.* 2°. *This Lord and Master.* 3°. *My Lord and Master.* So Տէրդ և Վարդապետդ, 1°. *Thou who art a Lord and a Master.* 2°. *That Lord and Master.* 3°. *Thy Lord and Master.* Likewise Տէրն և Վարդապետն, 1°. *His Lord and Master.* 2°. *That Lord and Master.* 3°. *The Lord and the Master.* Զո՞յր զհետ ելեալ ես Ռաբբայդ

Իսրայէլի, *after whom is the King of Israel come out?* Տեղիս անապատ է, և օրս տարաժամեալ, *this is a desert place, and the time is now past.* Զի՞նչ իրք են՝ վասն որոյ եկիք, *what is the cause wherefore ye are come?* Եթէ ընդ փայտ դալար զայս առնեն, ընդ չորն զի՞նչ լինիցի, *if they do these things in a green tree, what shall be done in the dry?* Ա՛ռ դու զորդիդ քո սիրելի, զոր սիրեցեր զԻսահակ, *take now thy son, thine only son Isaac, whom thou lovest.* Արտաքին մարդս մեր, *our outward man.* Զի՞նչ իցէ 'ի մեռելոցն յառնել, *what the rising from the dead should mean?* Մեկնեցարու՛ք 'ի վրանաց արանց խստասրտացդ այդոցիկ, *depart* (I pray you) *from the tents of these wicked men.* Յարանցս յայսցանէ եկելոցս ընդ մեզ, *of these men who have companied with us.* Ո՞վ արար զխուլն և զհամր, զականին և զկոյր, *who maketh the dumb, or deaf, or the seeing, or the blind?* Եկա՛յք 'ի հարսանիս, *come unto the marriage.* Յոր եսդ իջանեմ, *in the midst whereof I dwell.* Յերիցունէ առ Գայիոս սիրելի, զոր եսդ սիրեմ ճշմարտութեամբ, *the elder unto the well-beloved Gaius, whom I love in the truth.* Զի ուր եմն իցեմ, և դուք անդ իցէք, *that where I am, there ye may be also.* Զոր դուդ առնես, *that thou doest.* Որում դու՛ն վկայեցեր, *to whom thou bearest witness.* Մինչ առ ձեզս եմ, *being yet present with you.* Զոր նայն առնէ, *what things soever he doeth.* Զոր սայս առնէ, *which this man hath done.* Տեսանիցէք զոր ընտ-րեացդ իւր Տէր, զի ոչ գոյ նման նորա յամենեսին 'ի ձեզ, *see ye him whom the Lord hath chosen, that there is none like him among all the people.* Ո՛վ է որ ասէդ ցքեզ, *who it is that saith to thee.* Ընդ որում և համար-ձակեալդ խօսիմ, *before whom also I speak freely.* Ո իշխանաց աշխարհիս այսորիկ ըդ-խափանելեացս, *of the princes of this world that come to nought.* Ո խայրդ այժմդ տեսա-նէ, *but by what means he now seeth.* Որպէս և կանխաւն ասէի, *as I have also told you in time past.* Իսկ յոր ոչն իցեն սոքա մերձ, կոյր է և զաչացու, *but he that lacketh these things is blind, and cannot see afar off.*

CONCORDANCE OF VERB.

The verb which is not a participle, or infinitive, is governed by a nominative, as, Իսկզբանէ արար Աստուած զերկին և զեր-կիր, *in the beginning God created the heaven and the earth.* Եւ երկիր էր աներևոյթ և անպատրաստ, *and the earth was without form, and void.* Եւ հոգի Աստուծոյ շրջէր 'ի վերայ ջուրց, *and the Spirit of God moved upon the face of the waters.*

The participle and the infinitive are often governed by a genitive, as, ՙՆախ ծնանին՚ մինչև է մտեալ առ նոսա մանկաբարձաց, *they are delivered ere the midwives come in unto them.* Ընտանեալ երկնից, և իջանել հոգւոյն սրբոյ ... և գալ ձայն յերկնից, *the heaven was opened, and the Holy Ghost descended ... and a voice came from heaven.*

In like manner are governed the preter-perfect, and the preter-plu-perfect tenses formed by a participle, and a substantive verb, as, Եւ ոչ գիտէր Յակովբ՝ թէ Ռաքէլայ կնոջ իւրոյ գողացեալ էր զնոսա, *for Jacob knew not that Rachel had stolen them.* Դարան գործեալ է նմա ՚ի նոցանէ արանց աւելի քան զքառասուն, *there lie in wait for him of them more than forty men.*

The accusative cannot properly govern a verb, but is subject to it, as, Եւ արդ որովհետև ազգ եմք Աստուծոյ, ոչ պարտիմք համարիլ ոսկւոյ՝ կամ արծաթոյ՝ կամ քարի, որ ՚ի ճարտարութենէ և ՚ի մտաց մարդկան քանդակեալ իցէ՝ զաստուածականն լինել նմանող, *forasmuch then as we are the offspring of God, we ought not to think that the Godhead is like unto gold, or silver, or stone, graven by art and man's device.*

The nominative of nouns agrees generally in number with a verb which is not a participle or infinitive, excepting those without singular number, or collective, as, Յարեաւ այլ ազգ, որ ոչ ճանաչէին զՏէր, *there arose another generation after them, which knew not the Lord.* Եկն միաբան բազմութիւնն, և խռնեցաւ, զի լսէին յիւրաքանչիւր լեզուս խօսել նոցա, *the multitude came together, and were confounded because that every man heard them speak in his own language.* Եւ ժողովուրդն ակն ունէր Զաքարիայ, և զարմանային ընդ յամելն նորա, *and the people waited for Zacharias, and marvelled that he tarried so long.*

The nouns joined with the conjunction և, *and*, sometimes agree, sometimes not, as, Եւ մեծացաւ այրն յոյժ յոյժ, և եղև նորա ոչխար և արջառ յոյժ, ծառայք և աղախնեայք, ուղտք և էշք, *and the man increased exceedingly, and had much cattle, and maid-servants, and men-servants, and camels, and asses.* Եղեն իմ՛ արջառ և ոչխար և էշք, ծառայք և աղախնեայք, *I have oxen, and asses, flocks, and men-servants, and women-servants.*

When the noun, or, pronoun is only one, the verb must be of the same person, as, Ես միայն մնացեալ էի, և սոքա ո՞ւր էին, *I was left alone; where had they been?*

When the persons are different the verb agrees with the first, as, Գալո՞վ գայցեմք ես և մայր քո և եղբարք քո, և երկիրպագանիցե՞մք քեզ, *shall I, and thy mother and thy brethren, indeed come to bow down ourselves to thee to the earth?* Յորժամ դու և նա միայն իցէք, *between thee and him alone.* Եթէ ես, և եթէ նոքա այսպէս քարոզեցաք, *whether it were I or they, so we preach.*

Sometimes the verb is supposed, as, Մեք կաւ, և դու ստեղծիչ մեր, և գործք ձեռաց քոց ամենեքին մեք, *we are the clay, and thou our Potter; and we all are the work of thy hand.*

The verb active governs generally the accusative, as, Եւ արար Աստուած զմարդն ՚ի պատկեր իւր. ըստ պատկերի Աստուծոյ արար զնա. արու և էգ արար զնոսա, so *God created man in his own image; in the image of God created he him; male and female created he them.* Եւ տնկեաց Աստուած զդրախտն յԵդեմ ընդ արևելս, և եդ անդ զմարդն զոր ստեղծ, *and the Lord God planted a garden eastward in Eden; and there he put the man whom he had formed.*

Sometimes the letter զ a sign of the accusative is supposed, as, Նա տայ ամենայնի կեանս և շունչ, և զամենայն ինչ, *he giveth to all, life, and breath, and all things.* Եւ առ մի ՚ի կողից նորա, և ելից ընդ այնր մարմին, *and he took one of his ribs, and closed up the flesh instead thereof.*

The verb active governs secondly another accusative, as, Զո՞ւ առնես զքեզ, *whom makest thou thyself?* Թագաւոր զայլ ասեն զՅիսուս, *saying that there is another king, one Jesus.*

The verbs active as well as the neuter and passive govern often their roots in the accusative, as, Սեր յաւիտենական սիրեցի զքեզ, *I have loved thee with an everlasting love.* Ամաչեսցեն զամօթ մեծ, *they shall be greatly ashamed.*

The verb passive governs generally the

ablative, as, Զի լցցի որ ասացաւն ՚ի Տեառնէ, *that it might be fulfilled which was spoken of the Lord.* Քանզի ՚ի պտղոյ անտի ծառն ճանաչի, *for the tree is known by his fruit.* Ճանաչեմ զիմսն, և ճանաչիմ յիմոցն, *I know my* (sheep) *and am known of mine.*

The infinitive sometimes is noun, and sometimes verb.

The preposition ՚ի put before an infinitive has often the signification of an adverb յորժամ, զի, *when,* as, ՚Ի տեսանելն զքեզ, բերկրեսցի ՚ի միտս իւր, *when he seeth thee, he will be glad in his heart.*

The infinitive or the gerund with its verb increases the signification of it, as, Ունել ունէր պարծանս, *he hath whereof to glory.* Միթէ թագաւորելով թագաւորեսցես ՚ի վերայ մեր, կամ տիրելով տիրեսցես մեզ, *shalt thou indeed reign over us? or shalt thou indeed have dominion over us?*

CONCORDANCE OF PREPOSITIONS.

Prepositions sometimes are put after the nouns; they change their places, and are redoubled, as, Ոյք հասեալ էին յԱստուծոյ իրաւանցն վերայ, *who knowing the judgement of God.* Մի ինչ պատճառս տալ հակառակորդին ՚ի հայհոյութեան աղագս, *give none occasion to the adversary to speak reproachfully.* Զհետ երթային բազումք ՚ի Հրէից անտի, և ՚ի պաշտօնէիցն եկամտից զՊաւղոսի և զԲառնաբայ, *many of the Jews and religious proselytes followed Paul and Barnabas*. Յամենայն ժամ զբարեաց զհետ երթայք, *but ever follow that which is good*. Յորժամ 'ի պէսպէս փորձութեանց 'ի մէջ անկանիցիք, *when ye fall into divers temptations*. Հատուցին ինձ չար փոխանակ ընդ բարւոյ, *that render evil for good*.

Adjectives are often used as adverbs, as, Մեծաձայն կարդացէք, *cry aloud*. Երագս ընթանային, և թեթևս դառնային, *they ran and returned*.

On the contrary sometimes adverbs are used as adjectives, as, Եւ էր նորա ոչխար և արջառ յոյժ, *and had much cattle*.

Negative adverbs ոչ, չ and մի, *no*, *not*, sometimes are put after verbs, as, Եւ խոզ՝ զի թաթաւերձ է, և կճղակս ունի, և որոճայ ոչ՝ պիղծ լիցի նա ձեզ, *and the swine, though he divide the hoof, and be cloven-footed, yet he cheweth not the cud: he is unclean to you*.

ACCENTS, OR NOTES OF PROSODY.

1°. Շեշտ or շեշտանշան (´) as, ծա՛ռ, բա՛ց, Ե՛ս, ճանաչէ՛, ա՛նդ, բա՛յց, ո՛չ, մի՛, ո՛վ, զի՛նչ ։

2°. Բութ or ըթանշան (՝) as, նախ՝ երկրորդ՝ դարձեալ՝ արդ՝ այնզի՝ այլ՝ ։

3°. Պարոյկ or ոլորակ (՞) as, ո՞վ, զի՞արդ, ո՞ւր ։ According to modern usage it is employed as an interrogative point, and as a note of admiration.

4°. Երկար (´), as, բա՛րէ, վա՛շ, Երու-սաղէ՛մ Երուսաղէ՛մ։

5°. Սուղ (°) as, հ°նազանդ, ը°նութիւն, Ա°րովբէ։ It is put on the syllable to make it short.

6°. Թաւ (՜) as, թիւ՛, թու՛ոց։ It is put by some moderns upon the letter ւ to mark its pronunciation as a վ։

7°. Ապաթարց (’). It is rarely used.

8°. Ենթամնայ, the mark of division of a word (‿).

PUNCTUATION.

There are three Points in the Armenian.

1°. Ստորակէտ (,)
2°. Մ՝իջակէտ (.)
3° Վ՝երջակէտ (։)

OTHER MARKS.

1°. Ս՝ակակէտ (’). It is put on the head of the letter ի, when it forms a preposition, as, ՚ի, առ՚ի։

2°. Պատիւ (՟) mark of abbreviation, as, Ա՟ծ (Աստուած). Ա՟յ (Աստուծոյ). Ք՟ս (Քրիստոս). Ք՟սի (Քրիստոսի). Տ՟ր (Տէր). Տ՟ն (Տեառն)։

3°. Սիւն (ı) which is one of the three columns of a ա entire; it is put sometimes to mark an entire ա, as, աշտıրակ (աշտարակ), պարıրակ (պարարակ)։

4°. Երկորեակ (") which marks the vowels omitted, or the words shortened, as, Ք"ղ"ք (քաղաք)։ Յով"Հ". (Յովհաննէս)։

5°. Փակագիծ ().

6°. Պատուագիր. The sign, or substitute of a word, as, ⁓ (աշխարհ)։

7°. Փակագիր, Cyper.

The letters of the Armenian Alphabet are used as the Numbers, generally with a line on the letter, so

ա̅,	1.	ճ̅,	100.
բ̅,	2.	մ̅,	200.
գ̅,	3.	յ̅,	300.
դ̅,	4.	ն̅,	400.
ե̅,	5.	շ̅,	500.
զ̅,	6.	ո̅,	600.
է̅,	7.	չ̅,	700.
ը̅,	8.	պ̅,	800.
թ̅,	9.	ջ̅,	900.
ժ̅,	10.	ռ̅,	1000.
ի̅,	20.	ս̅,	2000.
լ̅,	30.	վ̅,	3000.
խ̅,	40.	տ̅,	4000.
ծ̅,	50.	ր̅,	5000.
կ̅,	60.	ց̅,	6000.
հ̅,	70.	ւ̅,	7000.
ձ̅,	80.	փ̅,	8000.
ղ̅,	90.	ք̅,	9000.

NB. օ *and* Ֆ *being recent letters, are not included in the numeration.*

VERSE

The antient Armenian Verses or Songs were not rhymed, as the following for example.

Երկնէր երկին և երկիր, երկնէր և ծիրանի
 ծով.
Երկն'ի ծովուն ունէր զկարմրիկ եղեգնիկն.
Ընդ եղեգան փող բոց ելանէր,
Ու 'ի բոցոյն պատանեկիկ վազէր.
Նա հուր հեր ունէր.
Ապա թէ բոց ունէր մօրուս,
Եւ աչկունքն էին արեգակունք։

But now they are rhymed generally and are composed from five Syllables to fifteen. The following few lines are specimens with their own translation in prose.

of 5 Syllables.

Սէր անուն Յիսուս
Սիրով քով Ճըմլեա՛
Սիրտ իմ քարեղէն։

Jesus, whose name is a love, bind thou my heart of ston with thy love.

of 6 Syllables.

Եղեալ հարսն անմահին,
Երկնաւոր Փեսային։

Having been the bride of the immortal celestial Bridegroom.

of 7 Syllables.

Քաջաբար դու մըրցեա
'Ի հանդիսի ըստադին :
Valiantly fight thou in the public combat.

of 8 Syllables.

Սիրեա՛ զուսումն որով պատուիս
'Ի յերկնայնոց և 'ի յերկրիս :
Love thou instruction, by which thou wilt obtain honor from Heaven, and on earth.

of 9 Syllables.

Իսկաձեմ աղաւնի օդապար ,
Նոր Նոյեան տապանն է քոյդ դադար :
Thou dove, ever flying through the air, the Ark of the new Noah is thy dwelling.

of 10 Syllables.

Այսօր երևի անտեսն 'ի բարձանց ,
Բանին դպրութիւնք բոլոր եղականք :
Today the Invisible appears from on high; the knowledge of all creatures is discovered.

of 11 Syllables.

Բանաւոր ծառոց երևեցան ծաղիկք
Երփնազարդ գունով , անուշահոտ բուր-
մամբ :
Flowers of rational Plants appeared of various tints, and delicious odour.

of 12 *Syllables.*

Բոլորակ եմ կիսագունտ որպէս խորան ,
Բնութեամբ կայուն , անձամբ շարժուն , անտեսական ։

I am a hemisphere round as a pavilion, by nature firm, in reality moveable invisibly.

of 13 *Syllables.*

Գոչումն որոտման յետ հոսելոյն զանձրեւ կենաց ,
Ամփոփեալ յերկինս , առ Առաքօղն անդրէն դարձաւ ։

The roar of thunder having diffused the rain of life, is recovered to the heavens, returning to his Origin.

of 14 *Syllables.*

Բանիւ աւետաւոր բարառնաբար բարբառեսցուք
Առ քեզ եկեղեցի, դուստըր վերինըն Սիօնի ։

Let us cry aloud in joyful tidings addressing thee personally, O Church, daughter of lofty Sion.

of 15 *Syllables.*

Որ 'ի վերայ ջուրցըն գոլով ստեղծանէիր զարարածս ,
Իջեալ 'ի ջուրս Աւազանին , ծնանիս որդիս Աստուծոյ ։

Thou, who brooding on the waters didst make creation, descending in the waters of the Baptismal fount, dost give birth to the Sons of God.

EXERCISES

IN THE ARMENIAN LANGUAGE

ԹՈՒՂԹ ԿՈՐՆԹԱՑԻՈՑՆ

ԱՌ ՍՈՒՐԲ ԱՌԱՔԵԱԼՆ ՊԱՒՂՈՍ

(Գտեալ ի Մատենադարանին Հայոց՝ ՚ի Վարժէ Մխիթարեանց) ։

1. Ստեփաննոս և որք ընդ նմա Երի-
ցունք, Դափնոս, Եւբուլոս, Թէոփիլոս և
Քսինոն՝ առ Պաւղոս Հայր մեր և Աւե-
տարանիչ, և հաւատարիմ Վարդապետ ՚ի
Քրիստոս Յիսուս, ողջոյն ։
2. Որք ումանք երկու եկին ՚ի Կորնթոս՝
Սիմոն անուն և Կղէբոս, որք կործանեցին
քաջ քաջ զոմանց հաւատս, հրապուրողս,
և ապականեալ բանիւք ․
3. յորոց բանից վերայ դու ինքնին պար-
տիս հասանել ․
4. զի մեք ՚ի քէն ոչ երբէք լուաք զայնպի-
սի բանս, և ոչ յայլոցն առաքելոց ․
5. այլ այսչափ գիտեմք՝ որ ինչ ՚ի քէն
լուաք, և որ ինչ ՚ի նոցանէն լուաք, հաստա-
տուն պահեմք ։
6. Բայց յայսմիկ յոյժ ողորմեցաւ Տէր,
զի մինչ դու իսկ մարմնով ընդ մեզ ես, միւս-
անգամ լուիցուք ։

THE EPISTLE OF THE CORINTHIANS

TO ST. PAUL THE APOSTLE.

(Found in the Armenian Bible as an Apocryphal writing.)

LORD BYRON'S TRANSLATION.

1. Stephen, and the Elders with him Dabnus, Eubulus, Theophilus and Xinon to Paul our Father and Evangelist and faithful Master in Jesus Christ, Health.

2. Two men have come to Corinth, Simon by name and Clebus, who vehemently disturb the faith of some with deceitful and corrupt words;
3. of which words thou should'st inform thyself:
4. for neither have we heard such words from thee, nor from the other apostles:
5. but we know only that what we have heard from thee and from them, we have kept firmly.
6. But in this chiefly has our Lord had compassion, that, whilst thou art yet with us in the flesh, we are again about to hear from thee.

7. Արդ՝ կամ գրեա՛ դու առ մեզ, եւ
կամ ինքնին դո՛ւ առ մեզ վաղվաղակի ե-
կեսջիր.

8. մեք հաւատամք 'ի Տէր՝ թէ որպէս
յայտնութիւն ցուցաւ Թէոնոնեայ, եթէ
փրկեաց զքեզ Տէր 'ի ձեռաց անօրինին։

9. Եւ են բանք մոլորութեան պղծոցն՝
զոր ասենն եւ ուսուցանենն, այսպէս։

10. Չէ՛ պարտ ասեն զՄարգարէսն ըն-
դունել.

11. եւ ո՛չ Աստուած ասեն ամենակալ։

12. եւ ո՛չ ասեն յարութիւն մարմնոց մե-
ռելոց.

13. եւ ո՛չ զմարդն ասեն, բնաւ ստեղծեալ
յԱստուծոյ.

14. եւ ո՛չ 'ի Կուսէն Մարիամայ ծնեալ
ասեն զՅիսուս Քրիստոս մարմնով.

15. եւ ո՛չ զաշխարհս արարած ասեն Աս-
տուծոյ, այլ հրեշտակի ուրումն։

16. Արդ՝ փո՛յթ յանձին կալջիր հասանել
առ մեզ։

17. զի առանց գայթակղութեան կայցէ
քաղաքս Կորնթացւոց.

18. եւ նոցա յիմարութիւնն յայտ յանդի-
մանութեամբ ամենեցուն խայտառակեալ
մերժեսցին։ Ո՛ղջ լեր։

19. Առին, տարան զթուղթն Սարկա-
ւագք 'ի քաղաքն Փիլիպեցւոց՝ Թերեպտոս
եւ Տիքոս. զի իբրեւ առ զայն թուղթն Պաւ-
ղոս՝ թէպէտ եւ ինքն 'ի կապանս էր վասն

7. Therefore do thou write to us, or come thyself amongst us quickly :

8. we believe in the Lord, that, as it was revealed to Theonas, he hath delivered thee from the hands of the unrighteous.

9. But these are the sinful words of these impure men, for thus do they say and teach.

10. that it behoves not to admit the Prophets:

11. neither do they affirm the omnipotence of God:

12. neither do they affirm the resurrection of the flesh:

13. neither do they affirm that man was altogether created by God:

14. neither do they affirm that Jesus Christ was born in the flesh from the Virgin Mary:

15. neither do they affirm that the world was the work of God, but of some one of the Angels.

16. Therefore do thou make haste to come amongst us:

17. that this city of the Corinthians may remain without scandal:

18. and that the folly of these men may be made manifest by an open refutation; Fare thee well.

19. The Deacons Thereptus and Tichus received and conveyed the epistle to the City of the Philippians. When Paul received the epistle although he was then in chains on ac-

Ստատոնիկեայ Ապոփողանի կնոջ, իբրև մուանալ նմա զկապանս, և սուգ առնուլ նմա վասն բանիցն զոր լուաւ։ և ասէ լալով, իբրև թէ լաւ էր ինձ եթէ վախճանեալ էի՝ և ընդ Տեառն էի, քան թէ ասէին նորին մարմնով, և զայնպիսի բանս և զաղէտս լսեմ զսուտ վարդապետութեան, զի տրտմութի՛ւն 'ի տրտմութեան վերայ հասանէ աւադիկ։ Եւ յայդչափ տառապանաց վերայ կալ 'ի կապանս, և տեսանել զայդ աղէտ տարակոյս, առ որս ընթացեալ սատանայի և մեքենայից նորա, գործել հնարի զչարիս։ Եւ այսպէս բազում չարչարանօք առնէր Պաւղոս թղթոյն պատասխանի։

ԹՈՒՂԹ ՊԱՒՂՈՍԻ

ԱՌ ԿՈՐՆԹԱՑԻՍ

(Գտեալ յԱստուածաշունչն Հայոց՝ 'ի ճարգէ Անյայտեց)։

1. Պաւղոս կալանաւոր Յիսուսի Քրիստոսի առ եղբարս Կորնթացիս, 'ի բազում վրիպակէ ասաի ողջոյն։

2. Ես ոչինչ կարի զարմացեալ եմ՝ եթէ այդչափ վաղվաղակի ընթանան հրապոյրք չարին։

count of Statonice the wife of Apopholanus, yet as it were forgetting his bonds, he mourned over these words, and said weeping:—It were better for me to be dead, and with the Lord. For while I am in this body, and hear the wretched words of such false doctrine; behold, grief arises upon grief, and this trouble adds a weight to my chains, when I behold this calamity, and progress of the machinations of Satan, who searcheth to do wrong.—And thus with deep affliction Paul composed his reply to the epistle.

EPISTLE OF PAUL

TO THE CORINTHIANS.

(Found in the Armenian-Bible as an Apocryphal writing.)

LORD BYRON'S TRANSLATION.

1. Paul in bonds for Jesus Christ, disturbed by so many errors, to his Corinthian brethren, Health.

2. I nothing marvel that the preachers of evil have made this progress.

3. Այլ զի Տէր Յիսուս վաղվաղակի ա-
ռաքեաց զգալուստն իւր վասն այնորիկ՝ որ փո-
փոխեն և անարգեն զհրամանս նորա ։
4. Այլ ես ինկզեանէ զայն ուսուցի ձեզ ,
որ ես ինքնին ընկալայ յառաջնոց Առաքե-
լոցն , որ զամենայն ժամանակս ընդ Տեառն
մերոյ Յիսուսի Քրիստոսի շրջէին ։
5. Եւ արդ՝ ասեմ, զի Տէր Յիսուս Քրիս-
տոս 'ի Մարիամայ Կուսէ ծնաւ , որ էր 'ի
զաւակէն Դաւթի ,
6. ըստ աւետեաց Հոգւոյն Սրբոյ, առ 'ի
Հօրէ 'ի յերկնից առաքելոյ 'ի նմա .

7. զի յաշխարհս մնեացի Յիսուս , և ազա-
տեացէ զամենայն մարմին իւրով մարմնովն .
զի զմեզ 'ի մեռելոց յարուսցէ .
8. որպէս եցոյց զանձն օրինակ ։
9. Եւ զի յայտ լիցի զի մարդն 'ի Հօրէ
ստեղծաւ ։
10. վասն այնորիկ մարդն 'ի կորստեանն
իւրում անխնդիր ոչ մնաց ,
11. այլ խնդրեցաւ , զի 'ի ձեռն որդե-
գրութեանն կենդանասցի ։
12. Քանզի Աստուած որ ամենայնի Տէրն
է , Հայր Տեառն մերոյ Յիսուսի Քրիստո-
սի . որ արար զերկինս և զերկիր , առաքեաց
նախ 'ի Հրէայսն զՄարգարէսն .
13. զի 'ի մեղաց անտի նոցա զնոսա կոր-
զեացէ , և հանցէ յարդարութիւն իւր ։
14. Զի կամէր նախ փրկել զտունն Իս-
րայէլի , բաշխեաց արկ նա յոգւոյ անտի 'ի
վերայ Մարգարէիցն .

3. For because the Lord Jesus is about to fulfil his coming, verily on this account do certain men pervert and despise his words.

4. But I verily, from the beginning have taught you that only which I myself received from the former Apostles, who always remained with the Lord Jesus Christ.

5. And I now say unto you that the Lord Jesus Christ was born of the Virgin Mary, who was of the seed of David,

6. according to the annunciation of the Holy Ghost, sent to her by our Father from heaven;

7. that Jesus might be introduced in the world, and deliver our flesh by his flesh, and that he might raise us from the dead; as
8. in this also he himself became the example.

9. That it might be made manifest that man was created by the Father,

10. he has not remained in perdition unsought,

11. but he is sought for, that he might be revived by adoption.

12. For God who is the Lord of all, the father of our Lord Jesus Christ; who made heaven and earth, sent first the Prophets to the Jews:

13. that he would absolve them from their sins, and bring them to his justice.

14. Because he wished to save first the house of Israel, he bestowed and poured forth his Spirit upon the Prophets;

15. որ զանմոլարն աստուածպաշտութիւն և զծնունդն Քրիստոսի քարոզեսցեն ժամանակօք բազմօք ։

16. Իսկ որ անօրէն իշխանն էր իբրև աստուածանալ կամեցաւ, ձեռն արկանէր 'ի նոսա .

17. և զամենայն մարդիկ մեղօք կապէր .

18. քանզի և դատաստանք աշխարհի մեռեալ էին ։

19. Աստուած ամենակալ իբրև արդարացուցանել կամեցաւ, և ոչ կամեցաւ խոտել զիւր ստեղծուածն ,

20. իբրև ետես չարչարեալ, ողորմեցաւ .

21. և առաքեաց 'ի վախճան ժամանակաց զՀոգին Սուրբ 'ի Սիոն, յառաջագոյն նկատեալ Մարգարէիւք ։

22. Որ իբրև սրտի մտօք հաւատաց, եղև արժանի յղանալ և ծնանել զՏէր մեր Յիսուս Քրիստոս ։

23. Զի կորստական մարմնոյն, որով հպարտացեալ յարդի լինէր չարն, նովին մարմնովն կշտամբեալ յանդիմանեսցի ,

24. Թէ չէր իսկ Աստուած ։ Զի 'ի մարմին անդր յիւր Յիսուս Քրիստոս կոչեաց և փրկեաց զկորստական մարմինն . և ձգեաց զնոսա 'ի կեանս յաւիտենից 'ի ձեռն հաւատոցն ։

25. Զի արդարութեան տաճար սուրբ յիւր մարմին անդր լինելոց ժամանակացն պատրաստեսցէ .

15. that they should for a long time preach the worship of God, and the Nativity of Christ.

16. But he who was the prince of evil, when he wished to make himself God, laid his hand upon them,

17. and bound all men in sin.

18. Because the judgement of the world was approaching.

19. But almighty God, when he willed to justify, was unwilling to abandon his creature;

20. but when he saw his affliction, he had compassion upon him: and

21. at the end of the time he sent the Holy Ghost into the Virgin foretold by the Prophets.

22. Who believing readily, was made worthy to conceive, and bring forth our Lord Jesus Christ.

23. That from this perishable body in which the evil Spirit was glorified, he should be reproved, and manifested

24. that he was not God. For Jesus Christ in his flesh had recalled and saved this perishable flesh, and drawn it into eternal life by faith.

25. Because in his body he should prepare a pure temple of justice for all ages;

26. յոր և մեքն իբրև հաւատացաք, ազա-
տեցաք։
27. Ապա գիտասջիք եթէ ոչ են նոքա
որդիք արդարութեան, այլ բարկութեան.

28. զի զողորմութիւնն Աստուծոյ կար-
ծէին յանձանց իւրեանց,
29. և ասեն, եթէ ոչ են երկինք և երկիր
և ամենայն արարածք՝ ձեռագործք Տ՟օրն
ամենայնի։
30. Այլ նոքա անիծեալքն զօձին ուսումն
ունին.
31. բայց դուք՝ զօրութեամբն Աստուծոյ
'ի բաց մերժեցարուք 'ի նոցանէ. և զխոտոր
վարդապետութիւն նոցա 'ի ձէնջ 'ի բաց հա-
լածեցէք։
32. Զի ոչ էք դուք որդիք անհնազան-
դութեան, այլ մանկունք սիրեցելոյն Եկե-
ղեցւոյ.
33. վասն որոյ ժամանակ յարութեան քա-
րոզեցաւ ընդ ամենեսեան։
34. Բայց որ ասեն՝ չիք յարութի մարմ-
նոյ, նոքա իսկ չեն յառնելոց 'ի կեանս յա-
ւիտենից,
35. այլ 'ի դատապարտութիւն։ Զի 'ի
դատաստան յարիցեն թերահաւատք մարմ-
նով.
36. զի զմարմինն զոր ասեն թէ չիք յա-
րութիւն, նոցա մի լիցի յարութիւն. զի
այնպիսիքն 'ի յարութենէն ուրացեալք գը-
տանին։
37. Նաև դուք որք Կորնթացիք գիտէք

26. in whom we also when we believe are saved.

27. Therefore know ye that these men are not the children of justice, but the children of wrath;

28. Who turn away from themselves the compassion of God.

29. who say that neither the heavens nor the earth were altogether works made by the hand of the Father of all things.

30. But these cursed men have the doctrine of the Serpent.

31. But do ye by the power of God withdraw yourselves far from these, and expel from amongst you the doctrine of the wicked.

32. Because you are not children of disobedience but the sons of the beloved Church.

33. And on this account the time of the resurrection is preached to all men.

34. Therefore they who affirm that there is no resurrection of the flesh, they indeed shall not be raised up to eternal life,

35. but to judgement and condemnation shall the unbeliever arise in the flesh:

36. For to that body which denies the resurrection of the body, shall be denied the resurrection, because such are found to refuse the resurrection.

37. But you also, Corinthians! have known

զցորենոյդ սերմանէ, և զայլոց սերմանաց .

38. զի հատ լոկ մերկ անկանի յերկիր . և
անդ 'ի խոնարհ նախ մեռանի .
39. և ապա յառնէ կամօքն Տեառն՝ զնոյն
մարմին զգեցեալ .
40. և ոչ եթէ լոկ մարմին մեկին յառնէ,
այլ բազմապատիկ տոհմականօք կանգնեալ
օրհնի :
41. Այլ մեզ պարտ էր ոչ միայն 'ի սեր-
մանաց անտի առակս 'ի մէջ բերել, այլ 'ի
պատուական մարմնոց մարդկանէ :
42. Դուք ինքնին գիտէք զՅովնան որդի
Ամաթեայ .
43. վասն զի յամառեաց նա 'ի քարոզելն
Նինուէացւոց, ընկեցաւ 'ի փոր ձկանն զե-
րիւս տիւս և զերիս գիշերս .
44. յետ երից աւուրց լուաւ աղօթից նո-
րա Աստուած, և ած 'ի վեր 'ի ներքին ան-
դնդոց անտի .
45. և ոչինչ ապականեցաւ մարմինն նո-
րա, և ոչ արտևան մի կորացաւ .
46. որչափ ևս առաւել վասն ձեր թերա-
հաւատք :
47. Եթէ հաւատայջիք դուք 'ի Տէր Յի-
սուս Քրիստոս, յարուցէ զձեզ որպէս ինքն
յարեաւ :
48. Ո՛վ եթէ ոսկերքն Եղիշէի մարդա-
րէի 'ի վերայ մեռելոյն անկեալ՝ յարուցին
զմեռեալն,
49. դուք որչափ ևս առաւել, որ 'ի մար-
մին և յարիւն և 'ի հոգին Քրիստոսի յե-

from the seeds of wheat, and from other seeds;

38. that one grain falls dry into the earth, and within it first dies;

39. and afterwards rises again by the will of the Lord indued with the same body:

40. neither indeed does it arise the same simple body, but manifold, and filled with blessing.

41. But we must produce the example not only from seed, but from the honorable bodies of men.

42. Ye also have known Jonas the son of Amittai;

43. because he delayed to preach to the Ninevites, he was swallowed up in the belly of a fish for three days, and three nights:

44. and after three days God heard his supplication, and brought him out from the deep abyss;

45. neither was any part of his body corrupted, neither was his eyebrow bent down;

46. and how much more for you, oh men of little faith!

47. If you believe in our Lord Jesus Christ, he will raise you up, even as he himself hath risen.

48. If the bones of Elisha the prophet falling upon the dead, revived the dead,

49. by how much more shall ye, who are supported by the flesh and the blood and the

ցեալ էք, յայնմ աւուր յարիջիք ողջանդամք
մարմնով։
50. Իսկ Եղիա մարգարէ զորդի այրւոյն
գերկս արկ և յարոյց 'ի մեռելոց.
51. որչափ ևս առաւել Յիսուս Քրիս-
տոս և զձեզ յարուսցէ յաւուրն յայնմիկ,
որպէս և ինքն իսկ յարեաւ 'ի մեռելոց ողջ-
անդամ մարմնով։
52. Ապա թէ այլ ինչ տարապարտուց ըն-
դունիք,
53. աշխատ ոք յայսմ հետէ զիս մի արաս-
ցէ. զի ես զկապանս զայս յանձին իմում
կրեմ,
54. զի զՔրիստոս շահեցայց. և կտտա-
նաց մարմնոյս այսմիկ համբերեմ, զի յարու-
թեան մեռելոցն արժանի եղէց։
55. Եւ դուք իւրաքանչիւրոք որպէս ըն-
կալարուք զօրէնսն 'ի ձեռաց երանելի Մար-
գարէիցն, և սրբոյ Աւետարանին՝ հաստա-
տուն կալջիք.
56. և վարձս ընկալջիք 'ի յարութեան
մեռելոց, զկեանսն յաւիտենից ժառանգեա-
ջիք։
57. Ապա եթէ թերահաւատ ոք լինիցի
և յանցանիցէ, դատաստան անձին իւրում
նիւթէ ընդ չարագործսն, և ընդ այնոսիկ
որ զայնպիսի առաջարկութիւն մոլորութե
մարդկան ունին, պատժին։
58. Զի նոքա ինքնին իսկ են ծնունդք
իժից և կորիւնք օձից և քարբից։

59. Մերժեցարուք և 'ի բաց մեկնեցա-

Spirit of Christ, arise again on that day, with a perfect body?

50. Elias the prophet embracing the widow's son raised him from the dead,

51. by how much more shall Jesus Christ revive you on that day with a perfect body, even as he himself hath risen?

52. But if ye receive other things vainly,

53. henceforth no one shall cause me to travail: for I bear on my body these bonds

54. to obtain Christ; and I suffer with patience these afflictions to become worthy of the resurrection of the dead.

55. And do each of you having received the law from the hands of the blessed Prophets and the holy Gospel, firmly maintain it;

56. to the end that you may be rewarded in the resurrection of the dead and the possession of life eternal.

57. But if any of ye not believing shall trespass, he shall be judged with the misdoers, and punished with these who have false belief.

58. Because such are the generations of vipers, and the children of dragons, and basilisks.

59. Drive far from amongst ye, and fly

րուք 'ի նոցանէ զօրութեամբ Տեառն մերոյ Յիսուսի Քրիստոսի։

60. Եւ եղիցի ընդ ձեզ խաղաղութիւն և շնորհք անդրանկին սիրելւոյ. Ամէն։

Արշակ մեծ Արքայն Պարսից և Պարթևաց, որ և ազգաւ իսկ Պարթև, ապըստամբել ասեն 'ի Մակեդոնացւոցն, և թագաւորել 'ի վերայ ամենայն Արևելից, և Ասորեստանեայց. և սպանանել զԱնտիոքոս Թագաւոր 'ի Նինուէ, հնազանդեցուցանել զամենայն տիեզերս ընդ ձեռամբ իւրով։

Սա թագաւորեցուցանէ զեղբայր իւր զՎաղարշակ 'ի վերայ աշխարհիս Հայոց. պատեհ իմն համարեալ այսպէս անշարժ իւրոյ թագաւորութեանն լինել։ Եւ քաղաք թագաւորութեան տայ նմա զՄծբին. և սահմանս հատանէ նմա զմասն ինչ յարևմտեայ Ասորւոց, և զՊաղեստին, և զԱսիա, և զամենայն միջերկրեայս, և զԹետալիա. 'ի ծովէն Պոնտոսի մինչև 'ի տեղին՝ ուր Կաւկաս յարևմտեանն յանգի ծով. և զԱտրպատական. ,, և այլ որչափ միտք քո և քաջութիւն հասանեն. զի սահմանք քաջաց՝ ասէ, զէնն իւրեանց. որքան հատանէ, այնքան ունի ,,։

Սորա կարգեալ զիշխանութիւն իւր մեծապէս, և հաստատեալ զթագաւորութին

from such, with the aid of our Lord Jesus Christ.

60. And the peace and grace of the beloved Son be with you! Amen.

LORD BYRON'S TRANSLATION

Arsaces the great King of the Persians and Parthians is said with the Parthians to have revolted from the Macedonians, to have reigned over all Assyria and the East; and having slain the King Antiochus at Nineveh to have reduced the world under his dominion.

He appointed his brother Valarsaces King of Armenia, rightly deeming that his dominions would thus become more secure and consolidated; he bestowed upon him the royal of Nisibin, and assigned the limits of his territory, one part from the west of Syria, and Palestine and Asia and all the inland places and Thitalia from the Pontic sea to the spot where Caucasus ends in the western Ocean, and Atropatane, and » whatever else thy prudence or valour may acquire. For to the brave, he says, their arms are boundaries, what they win, they wear «.

He, when he had completely tranquilized his kingdom, and established his power, de-

իւր՝ կամ եղև գիտել սորա, թէ ո՛յք, և որպիսի արք տիրեալ են ՚ի վերայ աշխարհիս Հայոց մինչև ցնա. զքաջա՛ց արդեօք, եթէ զվատաց անցեալ ունի զտեղի :

Նա գտեալ զոմն Մարի Աբաս (կամ Մարաբաս) Կատինայ, այր ուշիմ և վարժ քաղդէացի և յոյն դրով, զոր յղէ առ մեծ եղբայր իւր Արշակ արժանի ընծայիւք, բանալ նմա զդիւանն արքունի. և գրէ առ նա ձև բանից օրինակ զայս :

„Արշակ՝ թագաւոր երկրի և ծովու. որոյ անձն և պատկեր, որպէս և է իսկ, մեր Աստուածոց. իսկ բախտ և պատահումն՝ ՚ի վեր քան զամենայն Թագաւորաց. և մտաց լայնութիւն՝ որչափ երկնի ՚ի վերայ երկրի. Վաղարշակ կրտսեր եղբայր քո, և նիզակակից. որ ՚ի քէն կարգեալ Արքայ Հայոց. Ողջ լեր ամենայն յաղթութեամբ :

Զանգի պատուէր ընկալայ ՚ի քէն՝ քաջութեան և իմաստութեան հոգ տանել, ոչ երբէք անփոյթ արարեալ զքոյոյն խրատու, այլ խնամ տարեալ հոգացայ ամենայնի՝ որչափ միտք և հասողութիւն բաւեցին :

Եւ այժմ ՚ի քումմէ խնամակալութենէ զետեղեալ թագաւորութիւնս՝ խորհուրդ ՚ի միտ եդի գիտել, թէ ո՛յք ոմանք յառաջ քան զիս իցեն տիրեալ աշխարհիս Հայոց. և ուստի՝ Նախարարութիւնքս՝ որ աստ կան : Զի ոչ կարգք ինչ լեալ աստ յայտնի, և ոչ Մեհենից պաշտամունք, և ոչ գլխաւորաց

sired to know, who and what sort of men had reigned before him over Armenia, and whether they were valiant or indolent.

Having chosen therefore a Syrian, Maribas (or Marabas) of Catina, a learned man, and very skilful in Chaldaic and Greek literature, he sent him to his brother Arsaces, with proper presents, to entreat him to permit the inspection of the royal Archives; and furnised him with letters of which the following is a specimen.

„ To Arsaces King of Earth and Sea, whose form and image are like those of our Gods, but his fortune and fate above all Monarchs, and the greatness of his mind such as is the heaven above the earth; Valarsaces his younger brother and fellow-Soldier, appointed by him King of Armenia, sends Health and Victory in all things.

Since I received thy commands to cultivate valour and wisdom, I have never neglected this thine admonition; but have administered in all things with diligent care, to the extent of my capacity and power.

Being delegated by thee to this kingdom, I have resolved to enquire what order of men ruled over Armenia before me, and what was the origin of these Satrapies around me. For neither indeed appears any regularity of things here whence it may be seen, what was the worship in the temples, or

աշխարհիս առաջինն յայտնի է, և ոչ վերջինն, և ոչ այլ ինչ օրինաւոր. այլ խառն 'ի խուռն ամենայն և վայրենի։

Վասն որոյ աղաչեմ զքո Տէրութիւնդ՝ հրամայես բանալ զդիւանդ արքունի ընդդէմ առնդ եկելոյ առաջի քոյոյ հզօր Տէրութեանդ. զի գտեալ զզճալին եղբօր քոյ և որդւոյ՝ բերցէ զստոյգն փութապէս. և զմեր հեշտութիւնն որ 'ի կամակատարութենէ լեալ՝ քաջ գիտեմ խնդութիւն քեզ լեալ։ Ո՛ղջ լեր երևելիդ բնակութեամբ 'ի մէջ Դիից“։

Եւ ընկալեալ Արշակայ մեծի զգիրն 'ի ձեռաց Մարիբասայ Կատինայ՝ մեծաւ ըջմտութեամբ հրամայէ առաջի առնել նմա զԴիւանն արքունի՝ որ 'ի Նինուէ. միանգամայն և ուրախացեալ այսպիսի միտս ունել եղբօր իւրոյ՝ որոյ զկէս թագաւորութեան իւրոյ հաւատացեալ էր։

Եւ խուզեալ սորա զամենայն մատեանս՝ գտանէ մատեան մի հելլէն գրով. յորոյ վերայ էր՝ ասէ, վերնագիրն այսպէս։

»Այս մատեան հրամանաւ Աղեքսանդրի 'ի Քաղդէացւոց բարբառոյ փոխեալ 'ի Յոյնն. որ ունի զբուն հնոց և զնախնեացն բանս. որոյ սկիզբն լեալ ասէ զԶրուանն, և զՏիտանն, և զԱպետոսթէ. յորում և զիւրաքանչիւր ոք 'ի ծննդոց երից նախարարականացս այսոցիկ արանցս զարս անուանիս

what was first or last done in this region, nor are there any certain laws, but all is confused and barbarous.

For which reason I pray thee, my Lord, that to this man, who will abide in the presence of thy Majesty the ingress of the royal Library may be permitted that he may acquire the knowledge of such things as thy brother and son desires, and return to us with the truth. And the pleasure which is to arise from the fulfilment of our wishes, we well know will be a joy to thee also. Farewell, oh thou illustrious dweller among the Gods!

When Arsaces the great had received these letters from Maribas of Catina, with the greatest alacrity he permitted him to search the royal Archives of Nineveh, rejoicing that his brother to whom he had committed the government of half his kingdom, was endued with such a disposition.

When Maribas therefore inspected the Manuscripts, he found a certain book, in the greek character, of which this is said to have been the title.

„ This Volume was translated from the chaldaic language into greek, by order of Alexander, and contains the authentic history of the Antients and our Ancestors, who are said to commence with Zeruanus, Titan, and Apetosthes; in this book each of these three celebrated men and their posterity are

կարգաւ շարագասեալ՝ յիւրաքանչիւր տեղիս մինչև ցբազում ամս „ ։

Յայսմ մատենին Մարիբաս Կատինայ զմերոյ ազգիս միայն համեալ զպատմութիւն հաւաստի՝ բերէ առ Արքայ Վաղարշակ 'ի Մծբին՝ յոյն և ասորի գրով ։

Զոր առեալ ... Վաղարշակ ... առաջին իւրոյ գանձուն համարելով՝ դնէր յարքունիսն 'ի պահեստի մեծաւ զգուշութեամբ. և զմասն ինչ 'ի յարձանի հրամայէ դրոշմել ։

Յորմէ մեր հաւաստի 'ի վերայ հասեալ կարգի զրուցացս՝ երկրորդեմք այժմ քոյ հարցասիրութեանդ, ձգելով զմեր բնիկ նախարարութիւնս մինչև ցՔաղդեացւոց Սարդանապալայ՝ և ևս մօտաւորսն ։

Խորենացի 'ի Պատմութեան Հայոց ։

Եւ յայնժամ իբրև զփեսայ շքեղազարդեալ՝ էր տեսանել զձեռեալն յառագաստ իւր զՔրիստոս ։ Զայն արձակէր քաղցր՝ առ Կոյսն ողջախոհ. „Ընդարձակեա՛ զտեղի խորանի քո և զվրանից քոց, կանգնեա՛, մի՛ խնայեր. երկայնեա՛ զպարանադակս քո, հաստատեա՛ զցիցս քո. յաջ և յահեակ թռուաջի՛ր. և զաւակ քո զհեթանոսս ժառանգեսցէ. և զքաղաքս աւերեալս 'ի Կռապաշտից շինեսցես ։ Մի՛ ասէ, երկնչիր, թէ մինչև ցայժմ նորոք յամօթ արարի զքեզ. զի եր-

registered in order each in his proper place for many years «.

From this volume Maribas of Catina conveyed to king Valarsaces then in the city of Nisibin the history of our Nation faithfully compiled and written in syriac and greek.

When . . . Valarsaces had received this Manuscript ... esteeming it amongst his chief treasures, he directed the volume to be diligently preserved, and ordered a portion of it's contents to be engraven on a column.

Which narrative, we having verified the series of our facts, are now about to repeat at thy command, and to trace back our early government to the Chaldean Sardanapalus, and even beyond.

Corenensis in his Armenian History.

LORD BYRON'S TRANSLATION.

It was beautiful then to behold Christ as a bridegroom nobly adorned for the nuptial chamber, who spake with a soft voice to his most pure beloved: » Enlarge the place of thy tent, and of thy porch; spare not, plant it; lengthen thy cords, and strengthen thy stakes; for thou shalt break forth on the right hand and on the left, and thy seed shall inherit the Gentiles, and thou shalt renew the ruined cities of the Idolaters. Fear not, though till now by means of these I have co-

դուայ , և ոչ ևս զղջացայց 'ի քեզ բնակել հաճութեամբ՝ որ ես հանգիստ իմ յաւիտեանս յաւիտենից „։

Յայնժամ՝ որ վարանէրն գաղտնի՝ սկզբնաչարն թշնամին , ծանուցեալ՝ թէ մեքենայքն իւր խայտառակեցան , տիեզերք աստուածպաշտութեամբ ծաղկեցան , պատրեալքն դարձեալ փրկեցան , ժառանգորդք դրախտին 'ի հայրենիսն փութացան , երկրաքարշ հեշտութիւնն տեղի ետ , և երկնային սրբութիւնն պայծառացաւ , գործի ատելութեանն խորտակեցաւ , և պտուղ սիրոյն սկսաւ բազմանալ , յոյս ամենեցուն 'ի ստորնայնոցս վերացաւ , և յերկնային կայանն հանգեաւ՝ արտաքս սողէր յորջէն չարութեան , իբրև զառիւծ գոչելով շրջէր , բացեալ զկոկորդ չարութեանն՝ ջանացեալ առ 'ի կլանել զԵկեղեցին փրկեալ Քրիստոսիւ ։

Լամբրոնացի յՄեկնաբանութեան ։

Հանճարեղ շնորհալիդ ընտրեալ է ,
Յարքայից հզօրաց զարմէ է .
Մեզ պարգև 'ի տանէն Լատինէ .
Հրեշտակ հրաշագեղ Հռիփսիմէ ։
Սահահորդ ուղևոր երկնընթաց ,
Օրինաց երկնայնոյն խորագգաց ,
Ուրացեալ զանձն և զփառս հայրենեաց ։
Հրեշտակ , և այլն ։

vered thee with confusion. For I swear, that I shall never repent to make my abode of pleasure with thee who art my repose for ever and ever».

Then the first Enemy, in ambush for his prey, perceiving that his snares were discovered, and that the worship of God flourished throughout the world, observing that those who had been deceived were redeemed, and that the inheritors of Paradise returned to their country, that the celestial holiness poured forth it's glory, that the instrument of hatred being broken, the fruits of charity began to multiply themselves, and the hope of all no longer turned to the earth, ascended to the heavenly abodes, forth from the cave of his malice he issued like the lion roaring in his anger, and roamed about with open and insatiate jaws, to devour the Church recovered by Christ.

Lampronensis in his Synodical oration.

A. GOODE'S TRANSLATION

Ripsima! Angel surpassing in beauty, wisdom, and grace; thou art chosen from the family of mighty Kings, and given to us a present from the Latin race.

Thou travaller journeying on the road of heaven, well skilled in Celestial Laws, having denied Thyself, and the glories of thy native country. — Ripsima, *etc.*

Իմաստուն սուրբ կուսան գերյարգոյ
Հրով բանին 'ի յերկիր արկելոյ
Վառեցեր ըզլապտեր հաւատոյ ,
Հրեշտակ , և այլն :
Փեսային Քրիստոսի մարմնացեալ ,
Անապակ կուսութեամբ հարսնացեալ ,
Յառագաստ անմատոյց բազմեցեալ .
Հրեշտակ , և այլն :
Սիրասնունդ Սիրամարգ սիրալի ,
Նրբափայլ ոսկեթել տարփալի ,
Նռապակ իւղագլուխ ցանկալի .
Հրեշտակ , և այլն :
Իսկաձեմ Աղաւնի օդապար ,
Նոր Նոյեան տապանն է քոյդ դադար .
Օձասպան Արագիլ դու արդար .
Հրեշտակ , և այլն :
Մտաւոր Մարտիրոս մրցական
Իական Բանին Հօր զօրութեան ,
Ախակոխ քաջութեամբ ըզհրճնձան .
Հրեշտակ , և այլն :
Ի զունեղ թաթաւեալ 'ի բոսոր ,
Սաղարթուն կամրորակ իբր խնձոր ,
Հարսն ազնիւ դու արեամբ քօղաւոր .
Հրեշտակ , և այլն :

ՆԵՐՍԷՍ ԿԼԱՅԵՑԻ :

Wise, holy Virgin, most venerable, Thou didst light up the lamp of Faith with the fire of the Word shed abroad on the earth. — Ripsima, *etc.*

Of pure Virginity Thou hast been betrothed to the Bridegroom the incarnate Christ, and placed on the inaccessible nuptial couch. — Ripsima, *etc.*

Lovely Peacock! nursed affectionately, charming, delicately shining with thy golden thread; enchanting, anointed with thy triple crown. — Ripsima, *etc.*

Thou Dove over hov'ring in the air, the Ark of the new Noah is thy dwelling: Thou righteous Stork, who hast destroyed the Serpent. — Ripsima, *etc.*

Thou Martyr skilful and valiant of the power of the true Word of the Father, who didst firmly tread the Wine-press. — Ripsima, *etc.*

Thou art colored, having been plunged in a crimson dye; thou art covered with leaves like the blushing Apple; Thou comely Bride veiled with thy blood. — Ripsima, *etc.*

NIERSES CLAJENSIS.

Ի ՆՈՐ ԿՏԱԿԷՆ

Քանզի բազումք յօժարեցին վերստին կարգել զպատմութիւն վասն իրացն հաստատելոց 'ի մեզ՝ որպէս աւանդեցին մեզ որ 'ի սկզբանէ ականատես և սպասաւորք եղեն բանին, կամ եղև և ինձ՝ որ 'ի սկզբանէ զհետ երթեալ էի ամենայնի ճշմարտութեամբ, կարգաւ գրել քեզ՝ քաջդ Թէոփիլէ. զի ծանիցես զբանիցն որոց աշակերտեցար, զճշմարտութիւն։ ՂՈՒԿ. Ա. 1—4.

Առն միոջ էին երկու որդիք. ասէ կրտսերն 'ի նոցանէ ցհայրն. Հայր՝ տուր ինձ բաժին, որ անկանի յընչիցդ. և նա բաժանեաց նոցա զկեանսն։ Եւ յետ ոչ բազում աւուրց ժողովեալ զամենայն կրտսեր որդւոյն գնաց յաշխարհ հեռի, և անդ վատնեաց զինչս իւր. զի կեայր անառակութ՟։ Եւ իբրև սպառեաց զամենայն, եղև սով սաստիկ յաշխարհին յայնմիկ, և սկսաւ ինքն չքաւորել։ Եւ գնացեալ յարեցաւ 'ի մի ումն 'ի քաղաքացւոց աշխարհին այնորիկ. և յղեաց զնա յագարակ իւր արածել խոզս. և ցանկայր լնուլ զորովայն իւր յեղջերէն զոր խոզքն ուտէին, և ոչ ոք տայր նմա։ Եւ եկեալ 'ի միտս իւր՝ ասէ. Քանի՜ վարձկանք

FROM THE NEW TESTAMENT

Forasmuch as many have taken in hand to set forth in order a declaration of those things which are most surely believed among us, even as they delivered them unto us, who from the beginning were eye-witnesses, and ministers of the word; it seemed good to me also, having had perfect understanding of all things from the very first, to write unto thee in order, most excellent Theophilus, that thou mightest know the certainty of those things wherein thou hast been instructed. LUKE. I. 1—4.

A certain man had two sons: And the younger of them said to his father, Father, give me the portion of goods that falleth to me. And he divided unto them his living. And not many days after the younger son gathered all together, and took his journey into a far country, and there wasted his substance with riotous living. And when he had spent all, there arose a mighty famine in that land; and he began to be in want. And he went and joined himself to a citizen of that country; and he sent him into his fields to feed swine. And he would fain have filled his belly with the husks that the swine did eat: and no man gave unto him. And

իցեն 'ի տան հօր իմոյ հացալիցք, և ես աստ-
սովամահ կորնչիմ. յարուցեալ գնացից առ
հայր իմ, և ասացից ցնա. Հայր՝ մեղայ յեր-
կինս, և առաջի քո. և ո՛չ ևս եմ արժանի
կոչիլ որդի քո. արա՛ զիս իբրև զմի 'ի վարձ-
կանաց քոց: — Եւ յարուցեալ եկն առ հայր
իւր. և մինչդեռ հեռագոյն էր, ետես զնա
հայրն, և գթացաւ. յարեաւ և ընթացաւ
ընդ առաջ, անկաւ զպարանոցաւն նորա, և
համբուրեաց զնա: Եւ ասէ ցնա որդին.
Հայր՝ մեղայ յերկինս, և առաջի քո, ո՛չ ևս
եմ արժանի կոչիլ որդի քո: Ասէ հայրն ցծա-
ռայս իւր. վաղվաղակի հանէ՛ք զպատմու-
ճանն առաջին, և ագուցէ՛ք նմա. և տո՛ւք
զմատանին 'ի ձեռն նորա, և կօշիկս յոտս
նորա. և ածէ՛ք զեզն պարարակ, զենէ՛ք,
կերիցուք և ուրախ լիցուք, զի այս որդի իմ
մեռեալ էր՝ և եկեաց, կորուսեալ էր՝ և
գտաւ. և սկսան ուրախ լինել: — Եւ էր
երէց որդի նորա յագարակի, և մինչդեռ
գայր, և մերձ եղև 'ի տունն, լուաւ զձայն
երգոց և զպարուց. և կոչեցեալ առ ինքն
զմի 'ի ծառայիցն՝ հարցանէր, թէ զի՞նչ իցէ
այն: Եւ նա ասէ ցնա. զի եղբայր քո եկեալ
է, և եզեն հայր քո զեզն պարարակ, զի ող-
ջամբ ընկալաւ զնա: Բարկացաւ, և ո՛չ կա-
մէր մտանել. և հայրն ելեալ արտաքս՝ աղա-
չէր զնա: Պատասխանի ետ և ասէ ցհայրն.
այս քանի՞ ամք են, զի ծառայեմ քեզ, և
երբէք պատուիրանաւ քով ո՛չ անցի. ուլ մի
երբէք ո՛չ ետուր ինձ՝ զի ուրախ եղէց ընդ
բարեկամս իմ, յորժամ եկն որդիդ քո այդ՝

when he came to himself, he said, How many hired servants of my ſather's have bread enough and to spare, and I perish with hunger! I will arise and go to my ſather, and will say unto him, Father, I have sinned against heaven, and beſore thee, and am no more worthy to be called thy son: make me as one of thy hired servants. — And he arose; and came to his ſather. But when he was yet a great way off, his ſather saw him, and had compassion, and ran, and ſell on his neck, and kissed him. And the son said unto him, Father, I have sinned against heaven, and in thy sight, and am no more worthy to be called thy son. But the ſather said to his servants, Bring ſorth the best robe, and put it on him; and put a ring on his hand, and shoes on his ſeet: And bring hither the ſatted calf, and kill it; and let us eat and be merry: For this my son was dead, and is alive again; he was lost, and is ſound: And they began to be merry. Now his elder son was in the ſield: and as he came and drew nigh to the house, he heard music and dancing: And he called one of the servants, and asked what these things meant. And he said unto him. Thy brother is come; and thy ſather hath killed the ſatted calf, because he hath received him saſe and sound. And he was angry, and would not go in: thereſore came his ſather out, and entreated him. And he answering said to his

որ եկեր զկեանս քո ընդ պոռնիկս, զեներ դմա զեզն պարարակ։ Նա ասէ ցնա. Որդեակ՝ դու հանապազ ընդ իս ես, և ամենայն որ ինչ իմ է, քո է. այլ ուրախ լինել և խնդալ պա՛րտ էր, զի եղբայր քո այս մեռեալ էր՝ և եկեաց, կորուսեալ էր և գտաւ։

ՂՈՒԿ. ԺԵ. 11—32։

Այր մի էր մեծատուն, և ագանէր բեհեզս և ծիրանիս, և ուրախ լինէր հանապազ առատապէս։ Եւ աղքատ մի՝ անուն Ղազարոս, անկեալ դնէր առ դրան նորա վիրաւորեալ. և ցանկայր յագել 'ի փշրանացն՝ որ անկանէին 'ի սեղանոյ մեծատանն. այլ և շունք եւս գային, և լեզուին զվէրս նորա։ Եւ եղև մեռանել աղքատին, և տանել հրեշտակաց զնա 'ի գոգն Աբրահամու։ Մեռաւ և մեծատունն, և թաղեցաւ. և 'ի դժոխսն ամբարձ զաչս իւր՝ մինչ 'ի տանջանսն էր, ետես զԱբրահամ 'ի հեռաստանէ, և զՂազարոս 'ի գոգ նորա հանգուցեալ։ Եւ նա աղաղակեաց և ասէ. հա՛յր Աբրահամ՝ ողորմեա՛ց ինձ, և առաքեա՛ զՂազարոս՝ զի թացցէ զծագ մատին իւրոյ 'ի ջուր, և զովացուսցէ զլեզու իմ՝ զի պապակիմ 'ի տապոյ աստի։ Եւ ասէ ցնա Աբրահամ. որդեակ՝ յիշեա՛ զի ընկալար անդէն զբարիս քո

father, Lo, these many years do I serve thee, neither transgressed I at any time thy commandment: and yet thou never gavest me a kid, that I might make merry with my friends: But as soon as this thy son was come, who hath devoured thy living with harlots, thou hast killed for him the fatted calf. And he said unto him, Son, thou art ever with me, and all that I have is thine. It was meet that we should make merry and be glad: for this thy brother was dead, and is alive again; and was lost, and is found. LUKE XV. 11—32.

There was a certain rich man, who was clothed in purple and fine linen, and fared sumptuously every day: And there was a certain beggar named Lazarus, who was laid at his gate, full of sores, and desiring to be fed with the crumbs which fell from the rich man's table: moreover, the dogs came and licked his sores. And it came to pass that the beggar died, and was carried by the Angels into Abraham's bosom: the rich man also died, and was buried; And in hell he lifted up his eyes, being in torments, and seeth Abraham afar off, and Lazarus in his bosom: And he cried and said, Father Abraham, have mercy on me, and send Lazarus, that he may dip the tip of his finger in water, and cool my tongue; for I am tormented in this flame. But Abraham said, Son, remember that thou in thy lifetime receivedst

'ի կեանս քում, և Ղազարոս նոյնպէս ըզ-
չարչարանս. արդ՝ սա աստ մխիթարի, և
դու այդր պապակիս. և 'ի վերայ այսր ամե-
նայնի վիհ մեծ է ընդ մեզ և ընդ ձեզ. եթէ
կամիցին աստի առ ձեզ անցանել, ոչ կարեն.
և ոչ այտի ոք առ մեզ անցանել։ Եւ ասէ.
արդ՝ աղաչեմ զքեզ հայր, զի արձակեսցես
զդա 'ի տուն հօր իմոյ. են իմ անդ եղբարք
հինգ, որպէս զի տայցէ նոցա վկայութիւն՝
զի մի՛ և նոքա գայցեն յայս տեղի տանջա-
նաց։ Եւ ասէ Աբրահամ. ունին զՄովսէս
և զՄարգարէսն, նոցա լուիցեն։ Եւ նա
ասէ. ո՛չ հայր Աբրահամ, բայց թէ 'ի մե-
ռելոց ոք երթիցէ առ նոսա՝ և ապաշխա-
րեսցեն։ Եւ ասէ ցնա. եթէ Մովսէսի և
Մարգարէիցն ոչ լսեն, և ոչ թէ 'ի մեռե-
լոց ոք յառնիցէ՝ հաւատասցեն։ ՂՈՒԿ. ԺԶ.
19—31.

Իբրև հրամայեցաւ մեզ նաւել յԻտա-
լիա, տային զՊաւղոս և զայլս ոմանս կա-
պեալս ցհարիւրապետ մի՝ որում անուն էր
Յուլիոս, Սեբաստեան գնդին։ Եւ ելեալ
'ի նաւ մի անդրամիտացի՝ որ երթալոց էր
'ի կողմանս Ասիացւոց, գնացաք. էր ընդ
մեզ և Արիստարքոս Մակեդոն Թեսաղո-
նիկեցի։ Եւ 'ի վաղիւ անդր իջաք 'ի Սի-
դովն. և մարդասիրութիւն ցուցեալ Յու-
լեայ առ Պաւղոս՝ հրամայեաց առ բարե-
կամսն երթալ, և դարման գտանել։ — Եւ
անտի ելեալ՝ խոնարհագոյն նաւեցաք 'ի Կիպ-

thy good things, and likewise Lazarus evil things: but now he is comforted, and thou art tormented. And besides all this, between us and you there is a great gulf fixed: so that they who would pass from hence to you cannot; neither can they pass to us that would come from thence. Then he said, I pray thee therefore, father, that thou wouldest send him to my father's house; for I have five brethren: that he may testify unto them, lest they also come into this place of torment. Abraham saith unto him, They have Moses, and the prophets; let them hear them. And he said, Nay, father Abraham: but if one went unto them from the dead, they will repent. And he said unto him, If they hear not Moses and the prophets, neither will they be persuaded though one rose from the dead. LUKE XVI. 19—31.

When it was determined that we should sail into Italy, they delivered Paul and certain other prisoners unto one named Julius, a centurion of Augustus' band. And entering into a ship of Adramyttium, we launched, meaning to sail by the coasts of Asia; one Aristarchus, a Macedonian of Thessalonica, being with us. And the next day we touched at Sidon. And Julius courteously entreated Paul, and gave him liberty to go unto his friends to refresh himself. — And when we had launched from thence, we sail-

րոս, վասն հողմոյն ընդդէմ լինելոյ։ Յայն ժամ ընդ մէջ ծովուն Կիլիկեայ և Պամփիլեայ նաւեալ՝ իջաք 'ի Միւռա Լիկիացւոց։ Եւ անդ գտեալ հարիւրապետին զնաւ մի աղէքսանդրացի՝ որ երթայր յԻտալիա, եմոյծ զմեզ անդր։ Եւ 'ի բազում աւուրս ծանրանաւեալք՝ հազիւ հասաք առ Կնիդաւ. և 'ի չթողացուցանել մեզ հողմոյն՝ նաւեցաք խոնարհագոյն 'ի Կրետէ առ Սաղմոնեաւ։ Հազիւ անցեալ առ նովաւ՝ եկաք 'ի տեղի ինչ, որ կոչէր Գեղեցիկ նաւահանգիստ. յոր հուպ էր քաղաքն Լասեայ։ — Եւ իբրև բազում ժամանակք անցանէին, և սխալ ևս լինէր նաւելոյն, և վասն այն ինչ ևս պահոցն անցանելոյ՝ տայր խրատ Պաւղոս, և ասէր ցնոսա. Արք՝ տեսանեմ զի թշնամանօք և բազում վնասու՝ ոչ միայն բեռինդ և նաւիդ, այլ անձանց մերոց լինելոց է նաւարկութիւնս։ Իսկ հարիւրապետն նաւապետին և նաւավարին առաւել անսայր, քան բանիցն Պաւղոսի։ Իբրև դըժպատեհ իմն թուէր նաւահանգիստն առ 'ի ձմերել, բազումք խորհեցան գնալ անտի, թերևս կարասցեն հասանել 'ի Փիւնիկէ՝ ձմերել 'ի նաւահանգստին Կրետացւոց, որ հայէր ընդ հարաւակողմն և ընդ աշխարհն (χῶρον.). Եւ 'ի շնչել հարաւոյն՝ համարեցան ուր դիմեալն էին հասանել. և արկեալ մօտ անցանէին զԿրետէաւ։ Եւ ոչ յետ բազում ժամուց անկաւ զնովաւ հողմ ուռուցիկ որ կոչի Եւրակիկլոն։ Ընդ յափշտակել նաւին, և 'ի չհանդուրժել ընդդէմ

ed under Cyprus, because the winds were contrary. And when we had sailed over the sea of Cilicia and Pamphylia, we came to Myra, a city of Lycia. And there the centurion found a ship of Alexandria sailing unto Italy; and he put us therein. And when we had sailed slowly many days, and scarce were come over against Cnidus, the wind not suffering us, we sailed under Crete, over against Salmone; And hardly passing it, came unto a place which is called The fair havens; nigh whereunto was the city of Lasea. —Now when much time was spent, and when sailing was now dangerous, because the fast was now already past, Paul admonished them; and said unto them, Sirs, I perceive that this voyage will be with hurt and much damage, not only of the lading and ship, but also of our lives. Nevertheless, the centurion believed the master and the owner of the ship, more than those things which were spoken by Paul. And because the haven was not commodious to winter in, the more part advised to depart thence also, if by any means they might attain to Phenice, and there to winter; which is an haven of Crete, and lieth toward the south-west and north-west. And when the south wind blew softly, supposing that they had obtained their purpose, loosing thence, they sailed close by Crete. But not long after, there arose against it a tempestuous wind,

հողմոյն՝ թոյլ տուեալ երթայաք և գայաք. 'ի կղզի ինչ դիմեալ՝ որ կոչէր Կղաւդիա, հազիւ կարացաք ըմբռնել զմակոյկն. զոր առեալ՝ յօգնականութիւն կապէին ընդ նաւն: Երկուցեալ թէ դուցէ 'ի յորձանուտն անկանիցին, իջուցեալ զառագաստն այնպէս երթային և գային: Եւ 'ի սաստկագոյն վըրտանալոյն մերոյ՝ 'ի վաղիւ անդր զկարասին ընկեցիկ առնէին. և յերրիր աւուր ընդ իրեանց ձեռն զգործին նաւին ընկեցին: — Իբրև ոչ արև, և ոչ աստեղք երևէին 'ի բազում աւուրս, և ձմեռն ոչ սակաւ կայր 'ի վերայ՝ ապա բառնայր ամենայն յոյս փըրկութեան մերոյ: Եւ զի բազում աւուրս նօթի էին, յայնժամ Պաւղոս կացեալ 'ի մէջ նոցա ասէ. Պա՛րտ էր ձեզ՝ ո՛վ արք, անսալ ինձ, և ոչ ելանել 'ի Կրետեայ, և շահել զվիշտս զայս և զխասս. և արդ՝ խրատեմ զձեզ քաջալերել, զի վնաս անձին և ոչ միում 'ի ձէնջ լինիցի՝ բաց 'ի նաւէդ. քանզի երևեցաւ ինձ յայսմ գիշերի Հրեշտակ Աստուծոյ՝ որոյ եսն եմ, և պաշտեմ զնա. և ասէ. Մ՛ի երկնչիր Պաւղէ, Կայսեր ես պարտ է քեզ յանդիման լինել. և ահա շնորհեալ է քեզ Աստուծոյ զամենեսեան՝ որ են ընդ քեզ 'ի նաւիդ: Վասն այսորիկ քաջալերեցարո՛ւք արք, զի հաւատամ յԱստուած, թէ այսպէս լինի՝ զոր օրինակ խօսեցաւ ընդ իս, բայց 'ի կղզի ինչ հասանէ մեզ անկանել: — Իբրև չորեքտասաներորդ գիշեր լինէր, մինչդեռ ծփէաք 'ի Հանդրին անդունդս՝ 'ի մէջ գիշերին կարծէին նաւավարքն, եթէ հասեալ

called Euroclydon. And when the ship was caught, and could not bear up into the wind, we let her drive. And running under a certain island which is called Clauda, we had much work to come by the boat; which when they had taken up, they used helps, undergirding the ship; and fearing lest they should fall into the quicksands, strake sail, and so were driven: And we being exceedingly tossed with a tempest, the next day they lightened the ship; and the third day we cast out with our own hands the tackling of the ship. — And when neither sun nor stars in many days appeared, and no small tempest lay on us, all hope that we should be saved was then taken away. But after long abstinence, Paul stood forth in the midst of them, and said, Sirs, ye should have hearkened unto me, and not have loosed from Crete, and to have gained this harm and loss. And now I exhort you to be of good cheer: for there shall be no loss of any man's life among you, but of the ship. For there stood by me this night the Angel of God, whose I am, and whom I serve, saying, Fear not, Paul; thou must be brought before Cesar: and, lo, God hath given thee all them who sail with thee. Wherefore, sirs, be of good cheer; for I believe God, that it shall be even as it was told me. Howbeit, we must be cast upon a certain island. — But when the fourteenth night was come, as we were driven up and

իցեն յաշխարհ ուրեք . և ընկեցեալ ըղ-
գունտամն՝ գտին գիրկս քսան . և սակաւ ինչ
դադարեալ՝ դարձեալ ընկեցին , և գտին
գիրկս հնգետասան ։ Զահի հարեալ թէ
գուցէ 'ի խիստ ինչ տեղիս անկանիցին , յե-
տուստ կողմանէ ընկեցին խարիսխս չորս . ըղ-
ձանային այգուն լինելոյ ։ Բայց նաւավարքն
խնդրէին փախչել 'ի նաւէ անտի , և իջու-
ցեալ զկուրն 'ի ծով անդր պատճառանօք՝
որպէս թէ յառաջոյ կողմանէ խարիսխս ձգե-
լոց իցեն ։ Ասէ Պաւղոս ցհարիւրապետն ,
և ցզօրականսն . Եթէ ոչ դոքա մնան 'ի նա-
ւիս , դուք ապրել ոչ կարէք ։ Յայնժամ զօ-
րականք հատին զլարս կրին , և 'ի բաց ըն-
կեցին ։ — Եւ մինչդեռ այգն կամէր լինել ,
աղաչէր Պաւղոս զամենեսեան առնուլ կե-
րակուր , ասէ . Այս չորեքտասաներորդ օր
է՝ որում ակն ունիք նօթիս կատարել , և
չէ ինչ ճաշակեալ . վասն որոյ աղաչեմ զձեզ
ճաշակել կերակուր , զի այն իսկ վասն ձե-
րոյ փրկութեան է . զի ոչ ուրուք 'ի ձէնջ
մազ մի 'ի գլխոյ կորիցէ ։ Եւ իբրև ասաց
զայս , առեալ հաց՝ գոհացաւ զԱստուծոյ ա-
ռաջի ամենեցուն . եբեկ , և սկսաւ ուտել ։
Եւ քաջալերեցան ամենեքին , և նոքա առին
կերակուր ։ Եւ էաք ամենայն հոգիք 'ի նա-
ւին՝ երկերիւր եւթանասուն և վեց ։ Իբրև
յագեցան կերակրովն , թեթևացուցին ըղ-
նաւն՝ թափեալ զցորեանն 'ի ծովն ։ — Եւ
իբրև այգ եղև , զերկիրն ոչ ճանաչէին , բայց
զպատ մի նշմարէին՝ թէ ափն ծովուն իցէ ,
յոր խորհէին՝ թէ հնար ինչ իցէ , զերծու-

down in Adria, about midnight the shipmen deemed that they drew near to some country: and sounded, and found it twenty fathoms: and when they had gone a little further, they sounded again, and found it fifteen fathoms. Then fearing lest we should have fallen upon rocks, they cast four anchors out of the stern, and wished for the day. And as the shipmen were about to flee out of the ship, when they had let down the boat into the sea, under colour as though they would have cast anchors out of the foreship, Paul said to the centurion and to the soldiers, Except these abide in the ship, ye cannot be saved. Then the soldiers cut off the ropes of the boat, and let her fall off. — And while the day was coming on, Paul besought them all to take meat, saying, This day is the fourteenth day that ye have tarried, and continued fasting, having taken nothing. Wherefore I pray you to take some meat: for this is for your health, for there shall not an hair fall from the head of any of you. And when he had thus spoken, he took bread, and gave thanks to God in presence of them all: and when he had broken it, he began to eat. Then were they all of good cheer, and they also took some meat. And we were in all in the ship, two hundred threescore and sixteen souls. And when they had eaten enough, they lightened the ship, and cast out the wheat into the sea. —And when it was day,

ցանել զնաւն ։ Եւ զխարիսխսն հատեալ՝ ըն-
կեցին 'ի ծովն . Թողացուցին զխառնելիս
թեւոցն , և 'ի բաց առին զառագաստն , և
ետուն հողմոյն յափն կոյս ծովուն ։ Ընկեալ
'ի տեղի մի երկծով՝ թիւրեցին զնաւն . և ա-
ռաջին կողմն նաւին խրեալ՝ անշարժ մնայր ,
և յետին կողմն քակէր 'ի բռնութենէն ։ Եւ
զօրականացն խորհուրդ արարեալ՝ զի զկա-
պեալսն սպանցեն , և զի մի՛ ոք լուղիցի և փա-
խիցէ . և հարիւրապետն՝ քանզի կամեցաւ
ապրեցուցանել զՊաւղոս , արգել զնոսա 'ի
խորհրդոյն . հրամայեաց՝ զի որ կարողն իցեն
լուղել , անկանիցին նախ , և 'ի ցամաք ելա-
նիցեն . և զայլսն՝ զորս 'ի տախտակս , և զորս
յայլ ինչ կահ 'ի նաւէ անտի ։ Եւ այսպէս
եղև ամենեցուն փրծանել յերկիր ։ ԳՈՐԾՔ
ԱՌԱՔԵԼՈՑ ԻԷ. 1—44 ։

they knew not the land: but they discovered a certain creek with a shore, into the which they were minded, if it were possible, to thrust in the ship. And when they had taken up the anchors, they committed themselves unto the sea, and loosed the rudder-bands, and hoised up the main-sail to the wind, and made toward shore. And falling into a place where two seas met, they ran the ship aground; and the forepart stuck fast, and remained unmoveable, but the hinder part was broken with the violence of the waves. And the soldiers' counsel was to kill the prisoners, lest any of them should swim out, and escape. But the centurion, willing to save Paul, kept them from their purpose; and commanded that they who could swim, should cast themselves first into the sea, and get to land: and the rest, some on boards, and some on broken pieces of the ship. And so it came to pass, that they escaped all safe to land. THE ACTS. XXVII. 1-44.

SELECT PIECES

FROM THE ARMENIAN WRITINGS.

Եղբայր ոմն Կերկեցի գնաց առ Հայրն Սիլովանէ, և ասէ ցնա. Հա՛յր՝ ոմն թշնախիմ է, և բազում չարիս գործեալ է ինձ. խլեաց յինէն զագարակ իմ մինչ էի 'ի գեղ, և մօգս և դեղիչս առաքեաց սպանանել զիս. և արդ կամիմ՝ զի տարեալ տացից զնա առ Իշխանն: Ասէ ցնա ծերն. զոր ինչ կամիս, արասցես որդեակ: Ասէ ցնա եղբայրն. Թո՛յլ տուր Հա՛յր, եթէ խրատեսցի՝ շահ լիցի անձին իմոյ և նորա: Ասէ ցնա ծերն. արասցես զոր կամիս: Ասէ եղբայրն ցծերն. արա՛ աղօթս, և արձակեա՛ զիս առ Իշխանն: Եւ յարեաւ աղօթել: Եւ իբրև ասէին Հայր մեր Որ յերկինս, ասէ ծերն. Մի՛ թողուր մեզ զպարտիս մեր, որպէս և մեք ո՛չ թողումք մերոց պարտապանաց: Ասէ եղբայրն ցծերն, Մի՛ Հայր, մի՛ այդպէս: Եւ ծերն ասէ ցեղբայրն. և ո՛րպէս որդեակ. այլ հաւատա՛ ինձ՝ եթէ գնաս առ Իշխանն դատել զօք, Սիլովանէ այսպէս աղօթեսցէ միշտ վասն քո:

ՎԱՐՔ ՀԱՐԱՆՑ:

'Ի հաւանութենէ արուին և իգին ըստ օրինաւոր ամուսնութեան կարգացն Աստուծոյ զաւակ ստանան 'ի սփոփանս անձանց և մերձաւորաց, և 'ի գովութիւն պարգևատուին: Եւ բազում ուրախութիւն ցուցանեն 'ի ծննդեանն, և բարեկամօք և մերձաւորօք տօն կատարեն ծննդեանն և անուանակոչութեանն. որ 'ի մթին և յաղջամղջին յորովայնէ յառաջ եկեալ՝ մարդ կերպարանեալ ցուցանի յերկրի: Եւ յորժամ սնընդեամբ մարմինն աճէ 'ի կատարեալ հասակ՝ պատրաստութեամբ արուեստիւք ոմամբք, և ոգիքն բանաւորք և միտաւորք ըստ մարմնոյ աճմանն զգիտութիւն և զիմաստութի̄ ընդունին բացայայտեն 'ի ձեռն ուսուցչացն իւրատուց. որ և պետութեանց և իշխանութեանց հանդիպին յերկրի: Եւ նախ քան զամենայն ճանաչելն զԱստուած, և արարածովքս իմանալ զԱրարիչն երկնի և երկրի, և որ 'ի նոսա արարածք իցեն: Եւ լինել աշակերտ և արբանեակ նորա կամացն՝ նմանեալ նորա բարերարութեանն. ատել զչարն, և ընտրել զբարին. և պատճառ լինել շահից, և խլիչ վնասուց կորստեան. երախտաւոր լինել հեռաւորաց և մերձաւորաց, առ դրացիս և ընտանիս՝ բարի կամօք և բարի գնացիւք և բարի գործովք. առ ամենեսեան լինել արժանաւոր իրաւամբք. և արդար և ուղիղ սուրբ և ճշմարիտ վարս ստանալ: Եւ այնպէս երանելի երևել յաշխարհի ամենայն առաքինութեամբ. զարդարել ըստ պատկերի Աստուծոյ: Փոխի յանուշակն կենդանի յանմահ փառսն՝ 'ի յոյն յարութեան. և ընդունի զերանութիւն սիրոյն։

ՅԱՃԱԽԱՊԱՏՈՒՄ։

Մի՛ 'ի լոկ ջուր և 'ի դատարկ հայիցիս յաւազան անդր Մկրտութեան, այլ շուրջ ջրոյն՝ և շնորհօքն խառնի Հոգւոյն սուրբ կենդանի։ Քանզի կրկին է մարդն՝ յոգւոյ և 'ի շնչոյ կարգեալ, վասն այսորիկ և սրբելոյն պիտի. զի որ անմարմինն է՝ անմարմնովն, և որ մարմնաւորն է՝ մարմնովն։ Արդ՝ Ջուրն սրբէ զմարմինն, Ոգին դրոշմէ զոգիսն. զի ցօղեալք 'ի սիրտ, և լուացեալք զմարմինն ջրով սրբով՝ մատչել յանդիման լինել առաջի մեծութեանց Աստուածութեանն կարասցուք։ Արդ՝ յորժամ իջանիցես 'ի ջուր անդր, մի՛ իբրև 'ի թեթև և 'ի դատարկ ջուր ինչ հայիցիս, այլ 'ի զօրութենէ Հոգւոյ անտի փրկութեանն սպասեսջի՛ր. զի առանց երկոցուն անհնար է քեզ կատարեալ լինել։

ԿԻՒՐԵՂ ԵՐՈՒՍԱՂԵՄԱՑԻ։

Եթէ երթիցես 'ի բժշկարանս, և մատչիս հարցանել, զամենայն դրեթէ զհիւանդութեան պատճառս անդուստ 'ի կերակրոցն գտանես. անտի բուսանին ախտքն։ Քանզի նուազ և թեթևախորտիկ սեղան՝ մայր է առողջութեան. վասն որոյ և մանկունք բժշկացն այնպէս անուանեցին. և զչափաւոր կերակուրս, և որով ոչն յագի ոք, և ըստ կարօտութեանն կերակրել՝ զնա մայր առողջութեան ասացին։ Եւ եթէ պակաս կերակուրն առողջութիւն գործէ, քաջայայտ է՝ թէ որ յագեցմամբ կերակրի, այն է արմատ հիւանդութեան. և ծնանի ախտս՝ որ 'ի վեր անցանէ քան զամենայն արուեստս բժշկաց: Քանզի ատամնացաւութիւնք, գլխադարութիւնք, և անբժշկելի ցաւք, ձեռաց խեղութիւնք և անդամալուծութիւնք, հողմք և դողդոջմունք, ջերմ յերկար և տաքութիւնք անչափք, և այլ ևս առաւել քան զսոսա՝ զի ոչ եթէ յամենայն ժամ լինիցին, և ոչ 'ի պակաս կերակրոց, այլ՝ յաւելակերութենէ և 'ի յագեցմանէ երևին և ծնանին այսոքիկ:

ՈՍԿԵԲԵՐԱՆ:

Ընդ Աստուծոյ և վասն Աստուծոյ խօսելով՝ ամենայն արթնութեամբ և զգուշութեամբ պարտիմք միտ դնել բանիցն ասացելոց, զի մի՛ ընդունայն, կամ թէ 'ի դատապարտութիւն մեզ ասացեալքն լինիցին: Ո՛չ թէ ընդ մեր նման մարդոյ ոչ դանդաղեալ մտօք խօսիմք, այլ իմացուածովք զբանն բերեմք, և յօդաւոր ասիւք պատշաճեմք, և մանաւանդ յորժամ ընդ աւագաց ունիցիմք խօսել, երկիւղալից մտօք բանիցն հոդ տանիմք, ապա որչափ անզբօս խորհրդովք ընդ Աստուծոյ, և ընդ Աստուծոյն պարտիմք խօսել, և ամենայն երկիւղիւ ընդ նմա և վասն նորա բանաւոր իմացուածովք աւարտել զբանսն:

ՄԵԾՆ ԽՈՍՐՈՎ:

Չի՞ք ինչ շնորհ զոր առանց Առաջնորդաց տայ Աստուած : Այլ վերստին ծնընդեանն որ 'ի Հոգւոյն, և կենարար մարմնոյ և արեան Տեառն բաշխումն, թողութիւն մեղաց դարձելոցն 'ի խոստովանութիւն ապաշխարութեան, ամուսնութիւն զուգութեան, ընծայից և նուիրաց և պարգևաց մատուցումն, և հոգւոցն հանգուցելոց առ Քրիստոս յուղարկումն, և մարմնոց նոցա ընդ ամենապահ աջոյն Աստուծոյ ամրանալ, և որ այլ ևս կարգք են քրիստոնէականք, և օրհնութիւն Եկեղեցեաց Աստուծոյ, և սպասուց նոցա, և կամ նշանի Խաչին, կամ Միւռոնին գերագունի, կամ երկրի, կամ ջուրց, սերմանց, պտղոց, անասնոց, ախտից բուժելոյ աստուածային շնորհիւն, կամ այլ ինչ աստուածատուր պարգևի՝ միջնորդք Առաջնորդք եկեղեցւոյ լինին : Նոքա առնուն 'ի ժողովրդոցն զխոստովանութիւն, զաղօթս, զօրհնութիւն, ընծայս՝ և մատուցանեն Աստուծոյ. և դարձեալ՝ առնուն յԱստուծոյ զօրհնութիւնս և զզանազան շնորհսն, զխաղաղութիւնն երկնային, և տան մարդկան՝ մեռելոց և կենդանեաց :

ՆՈՅՆՆ :

Որ օրինակ թագաւոր ոք գիտելով ընծառայից զիւրաքանչիւր զքաջութիւն և զուժոյ կարողութիւն, նաև զպատշաճ պիտոյից գործառնութիւն ըստ ժամանակի և ըստ իրի, և առեալ կարգեսցէ ըստ արժանոյն՝ զոմն 'ի զինուորութիւն ընտրելով, ըզմիւսն 'ի դատաւորութիւն, զայլ ոմն դատաւորապետ կարգելով, և զմիւսն գլուխ զօրաց կացուցանելով. զմին 'ի դուռն արքունի կարգեալ, զմիւսն 'ի վերայ խահիցն, և զայլ ոմն մատռուակ և սպասաւոր իւրոյ թագաւորութեանն ընտրեալ. այսպէս իմն և ամենաթագաւորն Աստուած ըստ իւրում նախատես գիտութեան ընտրեաց զամենեսեան ըստ իւրաքանչիւր պիտոյից յիւրաքանչիւր դարս և ժամանակս ըստ արժանաւորութե՟ ։

ՆՈՅՆՆ ։

Յանկացայ զմարդն գործավասիրաց պահել սովորութիւն, առ որս տեսանեմք, զի կաթընկեր ունելով մանկունս, և անկիրթ ճաշակելիս կատարեալ կերակրոց՝ նախ ինքեանք առնուն զհացիկն, և յատամունս մանրեն, և ապա եդեալ 'ի բերանս նոցա՝ առ 'ի նոյնպիսի կերակրոցն ճաշակումն զտղայսն դաստիարակեն ։ Նոյնպէս և Վարդապետաց՝ որոց պաշտօն բանին հաւատացաւ 'ի Հոգւոյն, հարկաւոր է առնուլ զկատարեալ հոգւոց կերակուր՝ զգրաւորական վարդապետութի՟, և զնոյն յատամունս խաղաղութեան մանրել, և դիւրաճաշակելի և ախորժ առնել որոց կարևոր առ 'ի նոյն մնունդ և աճումն ։

ԴԻՈՆԵՍԻՈՍ ։

Զի որպէս յարեգակն պշնուլն պակասումն ընձեռէ աչաց հայեցողին, նոյնպէս և աւելի քան զչափն յառիլ 'ի խորս գիտութեամն Աստուծոյ շլացուածն մտաց աչացն բերէ ։

ՆԱՐԵԿԱՑԻ ։

Ոսկին համր է, և առանց բերանոյ կարող է խօսել, և լռեցուցանել զբանաւորս յիրաւանց ։

ՃԱՌԸՆՏԻՐ ։

Այոքիկ են բնութեանս մերոյ սահման․ յաղքատանալն տրտնջեմք և մեղադիր լինիմք Աստուծոյ, և 'ի հարստանալն ամբարտաւանիմք, և իբրև զանմահս զաշխարհէս բուռն հարկանեմք, վասն այսորիկ փոխ առ փոխ փոփոխմամբն ուսուցանէ զմեզ 'ի չափու ունել զանձինս, և քան զմեր սահմանն աւելի չամբառնալ՝ զի մի մեծագոյնս անկանիցիմք քան զհող անարգ և խոնարհ ։

ԼԱՍՏԻՎԵՐՏՑԻ ։

Նախանձեա՛ց ընդ մրջիւնն 'ի գործական առաքինութիւնն, և զմեղուն ա՛ռ տեսականին ապացոյց ։ Որպէս նա 'ի վերայ ամենայն ծաղկանց շրջի, նոյնպէս և դու զամենայն գիրս քննեա՛, և զպարկեշտն և զպիտանին 'ի նոցանէ ամբարեա՛ ։ Եւ յայնժամ զբանս հանճարոյ քո առնուն մեծամեծք և փոքունք 'ի բժշկութիւն հոգւոց, և քաղցր լինի 'ի քիմս մտաց նոցա քան զմեղու խորիսխ ։ Եւ այսու լիցիս ցանկալի իմաստնոց, և փառաւորիս․ որ 'ի տկար մարմնոյդ զերծուցեր զխոհականիդ բանականութիւնն, և իմաստութէն սիրով խառնեցար յանմարմնոցն կարգ։ Քանզի արդարև զմեղուի բերին զօրինակ Հելլենացւոցն իմաստունքն յաշխարհական հանճար, և եկեղեցւոյ Վարդապետք ՚ի հոգևորս գիտութիւն։

ԼԱՄԲՐՈՆԱՑԻ։

Որպէս նժար կշռոյ ունի անձնիշխան կամք կախեալ ընդ ինքեան զհոգին և զմարմին. ոչ պարտի տալ նոցա զմիմեանս հարըստահարել, այլ յօրինացն սահման պահելով զնոսա՝ ընդունելի է Աստուծոյ։ Ապա թէ հարստահարէ մարմինն զհոգին, ըստ ՚ի Պաւղոսէ. Գիրգն կենդանւոյն մեռեալ է։ Իսկ թէ ոգին զմարմինն, դարձեալ ասէ. Ո՛չ ջուր ևեթ ըմպեր, այլ սակաւիկ մի և գինի խառնեսցես վասն ստէպ հիւանդութեանդ։

ՆՈՅՆՆ։

Եւ վաճառք ըստ հրամանի Թագաւորաց կարգեսցին ՚ի քաղաքս, կամ յԻշխանաց ըստ հրամանի Թագաւորաց՝ թէ՛ ՚ի քաղաքս, կամ յաւանս, կամ յայլ ինչ տեղի ՚ի գաւառն. և նախահոգութեամբ զչափս և զկշիռս, ըղզոյգսն նոքա դիցեն՝ տեսանելով զզօրութիւնս վաճառին։ Կարգեսցեն և կափիչս՝ միշտ որոնել և տեսանել, զի մի՛ նենգութիւն ինչ արասցեն։ Այլ խարդախիցն խրատ ըստ հրամանի Իշխանացն լիցի. գողիցն ՚ի չափսն և ՚ի կշիռսն հատուցանել չորեքկին, և յանդիմանութեամբ նշանակել ՚ի զարհուրումն այլոցն ։ Իսկ դաշնեկանահատիցն և դրամափոխիցն զձեռսն հատանել հրամանաւ Իշխանացն ։ Իսկ զմաքսն առնու իրաւապէս , յորժամ 'ի քաղաքս կամ 'ի գաւառս եկեալ՝ վաճառիցեն . այլ մի՛ լիցի յանցս ճանապարհաց մաքսել , եթէ ո՛չ վաճառիցեն . այլ վարձս միայն , եթէ 'ի թշնամեաց՝ ընդ նոսա երթալով , պահեսցեն ։ Այլ մաքս հրամանաւ լիցի Թագաւորաց , և Իշխանք նմանապէս 'ի հրամանս նոցա մաքսիցեն ։ Այլ 'ի վաճառս խաբողացն զտգէտսն՝ ըստ գողոցն հատուսցի ։ Իսկ զգին հացի և զգինւոյ և զայլոց այդպիսեաց , ըստ քաջաբերութեան ամի , կամ ըստ այլ իմիք պատճառի , նմանապէս ըստ նուազութեան ։ Եւ ըստ այդպիսեացդ պատճառի փոփոխել 'ի վեր և 'ի խոնարհ՝ Թագաւորաց լիցի հրամանաւ , և Իշխանաց յիշատակելով Գաւառապետաց և Ժողովրդապետաց ։

ՄԽԻԹԱՐ ԳՈՇ ։

Այս իսկ է մարդ բոլորովին . ոգի և զօրութիւնք իւր , միտք և շարժմունք իւր , մարմին և զգայութիւն իւր . զոր պա՛րտ է ըստ վերագրելոցդ ամենայն զգուշութեամբ պահել . ո՛չ ընդ հրաժարեցուցեալսն ընտանենալ , և ո՛չ 'ի համարձակելոյն օտարանալ . զի մի՛ 'ի բարւոք և յընտանի կայից սաղօսկեալ՝ 'ի վայր քարշեսցի մարդն Աստուծոյ , և բիծ ինչ արատոյ ընդ անարատ մաքրութիւնն խառնեսցի՝ եղծանելով զնախատպին պատկերի լուսանկար գեղեցկութիւն ։

ԳՐԻԳՈՐ ՄԵՆԱՒՈՐ ։

Ասեմք զթիւսն նմանս գոլ՝ որոց կող֊
մունքն հաւասարք են, որպէս զվեցն, և
զքսան և զչորսն. քանզի կողմունքն վեցին
երկուք և երեքն, իսկ քսան և չորիցն չորքն
և վեցն: Եւ հաւասարութիւն ունի ութն
առ չորսն, և երեքն առ վեցն. քանզի կրկնա֊
պատիկ բանի տեսանի, զի չորքն երկուցն
կրկնապատիկ է, և վեցն երիցն:

ՆԵՄԵՍԻՈՍ:

Չարիւր և տասն ամ էր ՚ի Սրբոյն Գրի֊
գորէ, յորժամ գտաւ գիր ազգիս մերոյ. և
զայնչափ ժամանակս ՚ի յայլալեզու դեգե֊
րմանս էին տատանեալ. վասն որոյ առաւել
փոյթ յանձին ունէին, զի երագ վարժես֊
ցին մանկունք յիւրաքանչիւր տեղիս: Յո֊
րոց ընտրեցին թուով վաթսուն յաշակեր֊
տելոցն զառաւել ուշիմս և զփափկաձայնս և
զերկարոգիս, և առաքեցին յազգս և ՚ի լե֊
զուս օտար գաւառայ՝ ուսանել իմաստու֊
թիւն և արուեստախօսութիւն, և առնել
թարգմանութիւն ... որք գնացին յԱղեք֊
սանդրիա, ՚ի Բիւզանդիա, յԱթէնս, և յայլ
գաւառս՝ ուսանել զիմաստասիրութի որպէս
զայլ ազգս. զի նախանձ բազում էր յայնմ
ժամանակի ուսման ամենայն ազգաց, և ծաղ֊
կեալ էր ուսումնասիրութիւն յաշխարհի....
Զկնի բազումք յիւրաքանչիւր դարս և ՚ի ժա֊
մանակս հանդիսանային՝ նախանձաւոր բա֊
րեաց լինելով, ՚ի վաստակս և ՚ի ջանս պատ֊
րաստելով զանձինս. ժրանային, տքնէին, աշ֊
խատէին, հարցասէր լինէին՝ ուսանելով, կրթ֊

թելով, վարժելով, պատրաստելով զանձինս 'ի յերկս օգտակարս, և 'ի գործս շահաւէտս: Ոմանք զիմաստս հաւաքեալ՝ զուսումնականն, զբնաբանականն, զերկրաչափականն, զհամարողականն, զերաժշտականն, զաստեղաբաշխականն, զքերականն և զքերդողականն, զգործնական և զտեսական իմաստասիրութիւն, և զմասունս նոցա՝ որք են թուով երկոտասան.... Անելով ընդ ինքեանս բեռինս շահաւէտս և արդիւնաւորս, մարգարիտս գեղեցիկս և ականս պատուականս՝ զքաղխոհականն, զատենականն, զկացրդականն և զաստուածաբանականն՝ զարդարեցին զերկս աշխատողացն.... Ծանօթս առնելով բազմաց զգիտութիւն, զերևակայութիւն, զմիտս և զկարծիս, և զզգայութիւն, զարհեստ և զմակացութիւն, և զայլն ամենայն զգովելիսն և զպանծալիսն:

ՃԱՌԸՆՏԻՐ:

Մի օմն զօրաւոր 'ի զօրացն Հռոմոց պատրաստեալ հուրնաւթիւ ծծմբով, և արկեալ յաման ապակեղէն, և նստեալ 'ի վերայ ազնիւ երիվարի քաջասիրտ և արի գոլով, վահանաւ միայն զթիկունս ամրացուցեալ, և ելեալ ընդ դուռն քաղաքին՝ մօտանէ 'ի բանակն Պլազգեայն, ՄԱՆՏԱՏՈՐ ձայնելով զինքն. և երթեալ մինչև 'ի բաբանն, շուրջ անցեալ զնովաւ, և յանկարծակի 'ի վեր առեալ զշիշն՝ եհեղ 'ի վերայ բաբանացն. և նոյնժամայն բորբոքեալ հրոյն՝ բոց ծիրանի 'ի դուրս ելանէր, և ինքն դառնայր փութապէս ։

ԼԱՍՏԻՎԵՐՏՑԻ ։

'Ի սորա (փոքուն Թէոդոսի) աւուրս էր սուրբ հայրապետն Հայոց Սահակ. յորոյ աւուրս դպրութիւն Հայոց լեզուին՝ քսան և ինն գիր 'ի Դանիէլէ փիլիսոփայէ Ասորւոց կարգեցաւ. իսկ զեւթն գրոյն պակասութիւնն Մեսրովպ երանելի Տարոնեցի խնդրուածովք յԱստուծոյ առնու ։

ԱՍՈՂԻԿ ։

Կացոյց և լուսաւորս յերկինս՝ յառաջնորդութիւն և 'ի փոփոխումն աւուրց և ժամանակաց, 'ի մնունդ մարդկան և ամենայն կենդանեաց, և բուսոց և տնկոց ։ Նաև բղխեր և զջուր, զամպս և զհողմն յարդարեաց 'ի պէտս ազգի ազգի բուսոց և տնկոյ՝ որ 'ի պէտս մարդկան արարան իւրաքանչիւր ։ Եւ որ 'ի ջուրսն են ղուղակք և ձկունք, և ազգք գազանաց պէսպէս բնութեամբք և զանազան կերպարանօք 'ի ծովու և 'ի ցամաքի՝ մեծամեծք և փոքունք, քաղցունք և դառինք, շահեկանք և անշահք. Նմանապէս և 'ի տունկս և 'ի բոյսս՝ որ 'ի պէտս արարան մարդկան, և ոչ Արարչին ։ Արար և ոսկի և արծաթ և պղինձ և երկաթ. և պատուական քարինք և անարգք 'ի պէտս մարդկան՝ 'ի վկայութիւն մեծին Աստուծոյ արարան ։ Եւ 'ի չորից նիւթոց զերևելիս եցոյց. խոնաւ և ցամաք, ցուրտ և ջերմ յԱստուծոյ կազմեցան ։ Այլ 'ի նոյն նիւթոյ արարեալ զմարդն՝ և շնչեաց 'ի նա հոգի կենդանի և անմահ, մտաւոր և բանաւոր ։

ՑԱՃԱԽԱՊԱՏՈՒՄ ։

Ո՜ ինչ անգամ իցէ՝ որ ըստգիւտն համարեին 'ի սքանչելի արարածս մարմնոյս այսորիկ. զի՞նչ այն՝ որ պակաս ինչ է 'ի գեղեցկութենէ. զի՞նչ այն իցէ՝ որ ոչն ճարտարութեամբ կարգեալ իցէ ։ Իսկ արդ՝ ո՞չ է պարտ նոցա հայել և տեսանել աչացս լուսաւորութեանս զհաստատութիւնս, կամ ո՞րպէս ականջացն 'ի կողմանէ եդելոց անխափան զլսելիսն, կամ ո՞րպէս հոտոտելիքն ընտրութիւն գիտեն առնել. և զի՞արդ զհագագն 'ի տալ և յառնուլ՝ շունչ մատակարարիլ մարթ է. և կամ զի՞արդ լեզուն կըրկին կարգաց արքանեակ է ճաշակելեացն. և կամ ո՞ք ինչ ըստ ամօքելոյ բանաւոր խօսիցն զօրութեան. կամ շնչափողն 'ի ծածուկ 'ի ներքս ամրացեալ՝ զի՞արդ անդադար ունի զօդոցն և շնչոցն տալ և առնուլ մատակարարութիւն. կամ զի՞արդ սիրտն 'ի ներքս անդ միշտ անդադար զթնդիւնն պատրաստէ. կամ զի՞արդ յիւրաքանչիւր կարգս բաժանին երակքն, և նեարդք բազմացեալ ։ Այլ կամ ո՞վ է՝ որ խոնաւ ջղօքն և նեարդիւքն զոսկերս արար վայելչապէս. և կամ ո՞վ է որ զխորտիկս 'ի գեղեցիկ բաժինս բաժանեաց. զկէսն 'ի զօրութիւն հաստատութեան, և կէսն 'ի գեղեցիկ ընտրութիւնս խորհրդով բաժանեալ։ Եւ զամօթոյ մարմնոյն 'ի պարկեշտագոյն կողմանս թագուցեալ պահէ ։

ԿԻՒՐԵՂ ԵՐՈՒՍԱՂԵՄԱՑԻ ։

Որպէս ծարաւ յաղբիւր դիմէ յօժարական ,
Եւ ըղպաքեալ միտոք արբուցեմս բանիւք ուսմանն .
Որպէս լուսոյ ծագման յըստակ արեգական ,
Նոյն ըղհոգւոյդ աչըս բացցես տեսողական ։
Մ՛ի յայլասեր ազգաց գարշիր խնդրողդ ուսմանս ,
Մ՛ի յաղքատաց մեծամըտիր որպէս Իշխան.
Այլ ա՛ռ 'ի քեզ որպէս 'ի փշոյ վարդ հոտեւան ,
Թէ զոք անօթ շնորհաց տեսցես և պատուական ։

ԵՐԶՆԿԱՑԻ ։

Հեթանոսութեան սկիզբն 'ի Սերուքայ ժամանակաց անտի եղեւ . զի որ լաւ ոք եկեալ յաշխարհ մեռանէր , վասն յիշատակի քաջութեանն զպատկերն երանգօք 'ի նկարու հանէին . և անտի ուսեալ տխմարաց՝ տակաւ 'ի պաշտօն առնուին ։ Եւ կուոց և դրօշելոց հանգամանք՝ առ Թարայիւ հարբ Աբրահամու . և անտի իւրաքանչիւր ոք իւրով արուեստիւ զնոյն դրօշէր . դարբինն դարբնութեամբ , հիւսնն հիւսնութեամբ , արծաթագործն և պղնձագործ և քարակոփ և բրուտ՝ իւրաքանչիւր արուեստիւ ։ Եւ անտի կարգեալ հասանէր յԵգիպտացիս և 'ի Բաբելոնացիս և 'ի Փռիւգացիս և 'ի Փիւ-

նիկեցիս դրօշագործութեան, և խոր-
հուրդք նորին ։ Եւ ապա 'ի Հելլենս՝ որ են
Յոյնք, առ Կեկրոպեաւ. և ևս յետոյ ա-
ռաւել աստեղք առ Կռոնաւն և Ռէաւ և
Դիաւ և Ապողոնիւ, և առ այլովք բազ-
մօք՝ զորս մի ըստ միոջէ Աստուածս անուա-
նէին ։ Եւ Հելլենք կոչին Յոյնք յառնէ
միոջէ՝ որում Հեղլենոս անուն էր յԷլլադա-
ցւոց աշխարհին ։ Բայց այլք ասեն, եթէ
'ի ձիթենւոյն՝ որ յԱթէնս բուսաւ իւրովի.
վասն զի ձիթենի Յունարէն ԵԼԷԱ կոչի ։
Բայց Յոյնք 'ի Յաւանայ, որ էր մի յա-
ռաջնորդաց աշտարակագործութեան. վասն
որոյ ՄԵՐՈՎՊՍ ամենեքին կոչին յաղագս
բարբառոյն բաժանելոյ. քանզի Բաժանումն
Յունարէն ՄԵՐԻՍՄՈՍ կոչի ։ — Եւ առա-
ջին կրօնք՝ խուժականք և սկիւթականք և
հեթանոսականք կոչէին, մինչև եկն Աբրա-
համու աստուածպաշտութիւնն, և աղաւա-
ղեաց զայն ։ Եւ Յուդայութիւնն 'ի Յու-
դայէ՝ որ է Հրէութիւն, 'ի չորրորդ որդւոյն
Յակովբայ, յորմէ Թագաւորութիւնն էր.
և կալաւ անունն զամենայն ազգն Յուդայ-
ական ։ Եւ 'ի վախճանի Հրէութեան Քրիս-
տոնէութեան անուն 'ի Քրիստոսէ. որ նախ
յԱնտիոք անուանեցաւ աշակերտելոցն ։

ԵԶՆԻԿ ։

Զտեսանեմ և զմարմնոց իսկ աչս, յոր-
ժամ հանապազ ընդ ծուխ դայցեն, արտօսր
բերեն. և յորժամ 'ի խաղաղ օդս և 'ի մաքուր
և յաղբիւրս և 'ի դրախտս զբօսնուցուն, ա-

ռողջագոյնք և քաջատեսք։ Նոյնպէս և մըտացն ակն՝ եթէ յեզտիւրս հոգևոր բանիցն ճարակիցի, սուրբ, յստակ և քաջատես լինի. իսկ եթէ ընդ ծուխ ինչ աշխարհի իրացս գայցէ, բժաբեր արտօսրալից լինիցի. և զազգի ազգի լալիւնս լայցէ՝ և ասա, և անդ։

ՈՍԿԵԲԵՐԱՆ։

Չէ՛ ինչ ծանր հրամանքն։ Ո՛չ է ասա՛, զի՞նչ աշխատութիւն յերդմանէն փախչելն իցէ. մի՞թէ ընչի՞ց ծախք իցեն, մի՞թէ քրտո՞ւնք ինչ և տառապանք. շա՛տ է կամելն միայն, և ամենայն վճարեցաւ։ Իսկ եթէ զսովորութի՞ւն պատճառս դնիցես, նա՝ վասն նորին այնորիկ ասեմ դիւրին զուգութիւնն. եթէ յայլ ընդելութիւն կրթեսցես զանձն, զամենայն դիւրաւ վճարեսցես։ Օ մնաւած, զի բազումք իսկ ՚ի հեթանոսացն իմաստնոց՝ որ առ քաղթնատութեան թոթովէին, ստէպ կրթութիւն զկաղ լեզու նոցա էած յուղղութիւն. և ոմանք՝ որոց թիկունքն ընդոստ ընդոստ դողացեալ շարժէին, սուրս կապեցին ՚ի վերայ թիկանցն, և մերժեցին զսովորութիւնն։

ՆՈՅՆՆ։

Խրատեցէ՛ք զորդիս ձեր ՚ի խրատ և ՚ի վարդապետութիւն Տեառն. քանզի խակ և ամեհի է մանկութիւն, և բազում վարդապետաց կարօտ, դաստիարակաց, սպասկաց, դայեկաց. քանզի սխտոյ է այնպիսի վարժիւք վարժել ։ Որպէս ձի անեհի միշտ 'ի վարժոցս կայցէ, և գազան վայրենի 'ի հրահանգս՝ մինչև 'ի համբոյր գայցէ, այնպիսի է մանկութիւնն ։ Ընդստին իսկ յառաջին տիոցն պարտիմք սահմանս և կարգս բարիս հաստատել նմա. և ոչ եւս առյապա մեծամեծ աշխատութեանս կարօտանայցեմք. այլ սովորութիւն իսկ օրէնք լինիցին ։ Մի՛ տացուք նոցա թոյլ ըստ մտաց դիւրութեան գնալ, և մի՛ երբև մանկտւոյ ներիցեմք նոցա, այլ 'ի ցածութեան պահեսցուք. զի այն քան զամենայն ինչ վնասակար է մանկութեանն ։ Եւ մեք նմին կարի պատկառ կայցեմք՝ վաղ և արագ կանայս ածիցեմք, զի սուրբ և անարատ պահեսցին 'ի պղծութենէ՝ 'ի հասանել առ ամուսնութիւնն ։

ՆՈՅՆՆ ։

Որպէս 'ի մասունս մարմնոյ քան զամենայն պատուականագոյն և առաջին գլուխն է յաղագս տեղւոյն բարձրութեան, և ընդ գայարանացն 'ի նմա եղելոց, և ապա այլքն յանդամոց մի ըստ միոջէ. այնպէս և յանդամս հոգւոյն՝ մեծ և առաջին երբև զգլուխ, է հաւատոյն ճշմարտութիւն. և ընդ նմին յարմարեալք որպէս անձն ընդ գլխոյ, գործք արդարութեան մեծամեծք և փոքունք ըստ պատուիրանացն Քրիստոսի ։

ՆԵՐՍԷՍ ՇՆՈՐՀԱԼԻ ։

Հայեաց յերկինս 'ի վեր՝ ո՜վ մարդ, և յերկիր 'ի խոնարհ. և տե՛ս՝ եթէ զո՞ յարարածոցս յերևելեացս կամ յոչ երևելեացս այնպէս պատուեաց Աստուած, որպէս ըզքեզ։ Եթէ զառաջին պատիւ արարչագործութեանն ասիցես, ահա մեծ է և սքանչելի. վասն զի այլ արարածք հրամանաւն Աստուծոյ ստեղծան, և դու ձեռամբն Աստուծոյ։ Այլ արարածք 'ի պատկեր գծծութեան, և դու 'ի պատկեր Արարչին։ Այլ արարածք 'ի բնութեանն կապեալ կան, իսկ դու անձնիշխանութեամբ Արարչին քո նմանես։ Այլ արարածք անբանութեամբ անզարդք երևեցան և տրուպք, իսկ դու բանիւ և իմաստութեամբ զարդարեցար. և զպատիւն քո տիրապէս ոչ իմացար։

ՍԱՐԳԻՍ։

Զերկիր ոմանք յարտաքնոց բարեաց փիլիսոփայիցն ասացին, թէ ձևացեալ է իբրև սկուտեղ. և ոմանք ասացին իբրև զգունդ. և այլք որպէս քուէայ երկեռեակ դիմի, և 'ի միջոցի երկնի կառուցեալ. սաստկութեան հողմոյ 'ի ներքոյ մտեալ՝ համբարձեալ ունի զերկիր 'ի վեր. և ընդ անդայտութեան ցանկցիր հողոյն երկրի խառնեալ մանրասիկ խոնաւութիւն ջուրց, և հողմոցն սաստկութեամբ 'ի վեր փչելով, և երկրիս թանձրահող ծանրութեամբ 'ի վայր կալով՝ կախչի հողն յերեարս, և ձնշի իբր 'ի մամուլս, մանրասիկ խոնաւութեան ջուրցն կալով 'ի վեր կոյս. և խառնեայ երկրայինն մարմինս 'ի ներքոյ ջուրցն, և լինի սալայատակ, հաստատրամ, անփապելի և անպայթելի. նեցուկ

անվթար՝ զբազմութիւն ջուրցն յինքեան ու-
նելով, զոր և ծով անուանեմք։ Եւ քանզի
երկիրս չորեքկուսի 'ի միջոցի երկնի կառու-
ցաւ, ո՛չ թոյլ տայ սմա երկլին իւրով երա-
գութեամբն 'ի ներքին կիսագունդն խոնար-
հիլ. քանզի երկիր իւրով ծանրութեամբն
հակէ 'ի վայր իջանել, և հողմն իւրով ուժ-
գնութեամբն ջանայ 'ի վեր բերել զնա. և
ո՛չ ծանրութիւն երկրիս թուլացուցանէ 'ի
վեր բերիլ, և ո՛չ ուժգնութիւն հողմոյն տայ
'ի վայր իջանել. և այնպէս զհաւասարակշիռ
կէտն կալեալ՝ կայ. և յերկոցունց հակա-
ռակացն միջոյն զտրամագիծսն ունի։ Իսկ
կայեան սորա 'ի տրամագիծ անդր զուղղան-
կիւնսն չորեսին առ միմեանս հայեցուցանէ.
և 'ի հայել ուղղանկիւնեացն առ տրամա-
գիծն միջին՝ զամենայն հարթ, արդակ, զու-
գամասն՝ զլեռնայինն և զդաշտայինն և զծո-
վայինն յարմարեալ անշեղ պահէ, զի որ
'ի սմայքս են, անկասկած առցեն զլինելու-
թիւն հրամանաւ Արարչին։ — Եւ եթէ
ոք կամիցի օրինակ տեսական զարտաքնոցն
լսել, իբր թէ զկայս երկրի նմանեցուցեալ՝
ինձ 'ի դէպ թուի ասացեալն ձու. որպէս
նորա դեղլինն 'ի միջին գնդաձև կառուցեալ
կայ, և սպիտակն շուրջ զնովաւ, և խեձեպն
պատ առեալ զամենայնիւ՝ նոյնպէս երկիրս
'ի միջոցի կառուցեալ կայ, և օդ շուրջ զնո-
վաւ, և երկլին պատեալ զամենայնիւ։ Դար-
ձեալ՝ եթէ առցէ ոք աման խեցեղէն, և
արկցէ անդր ջուր, ձէթ և աւազ, ահա՛
յայտնի երևեցաւ՝ աւազն կալաւ զներքին

կողմն ամանոյն, և ձէթն զվերին, իսկ ջուրն հարկաւորեալ՝ ՚ի միջին կառուցաւ, և մարմին ամանոյն պատ առեալ զամենայնիւ։

ՇԻՐԱԿԱՑԻ։

Որ օրինակ՝ թէ ախորժէ ոք գծագրութեամբ դեղոց պատկեր նկարագրել, զպէս-պէս երանգս դեղոյն ՚ի կիր ածէ, և ջանայ ուշիւ իմաստիցն զնա ՚ի տիպ և ՚ի հասակ և ՚ի ձև կենդանեաց յօրինել՝ զի հաճելի և ցանկալի որպէս զկենդանի թուեսցի տեսողացն անկենդանին. իսկ մարդ կենդանի՝ որ կրի հոգւով, մարմինն ոչ այսոցիկ ճշգրտութեան երանգոց կարօտի առ ՚ի հրապարակել զիւրն կենդանութիւն. այլ բաւական է միայն հոգին ներգործող զշարժումն անդամոցն՝ զայս հռչակել։

ԼԱՄԲՐՈՆԱՑԻ։

Քաղաք ընտրութեամբ իմաստասիրացն տուրևառիկ վաճառացն տեղի սահմանեցաւ, որոշել ՚ի նմա տունս վաճառաց, և ընդարձակ վայրս։ Որ ի ամենայն գաւառականքն յամենայն կողմանց անդանօր ժողովելով՝ իւրաքանչիւր ոք զպէտս իւր գտանիցէ։ Բայց են և ՚ի մէջ քաղաքացն ընտրութիւնք. զի են՝ որ շահաւէտք են և բազմավաճառք որպէս ծովեզերեայ քաղաքք՝ որ զնաւահանգիստս պատրաստական ունին, և զնաւս բիւրաւոր բեռամբք ընդունին յամենայն կողմանց։

ՍԱՐԳԻՍ։

Որ երբեմն զհետ երամակաց ցռուց յանդնդագոյնս արշաւեալ ընդ խորտաբորտս և 'ի վիմուտ տեղիս, յորմէ կասել սկսաւ Շապուհ։ Իսկ Ատոմայ Մոկացւոյ եպերեալ զնա՝ ասէ. Դնա՛ զնա՛ աստուածորդի Պարսից, թէ այր իցես։ Եւ նա ասէ. Դու երթիջիր, զի 'ի քարինս դիւաց է շահատակել։ Դարձեալ՝ յայլում ժամու դիպեցաւ 'ի շամբս կինձս որսալ հրով. և Շապուհ ոչ համարձակեալ 'ի թաւուտն քաջարշաւ լինել, մինչև շրջապատէր հուրն. և նորա զհայեցուածմն յերկուս բաժանեալ՝ այսր անդր բերեալ լինէր երիվարաւն։ Միւսանգամ ասէ Ատոմ. Աստուածորդի՛դ Պարսից՝ ահա՛ հայր քո և Աստուած, ընդէ՞ր զանգիտես։ Իսկ Շապուհ ասէ. Թողեալ զկատակելդ՝ յանցանել ընդ հուրդ դարձ՛ զքեզ, որ և ես զկնի քո. քանզի յառաջելն ձիս իմ խրտչի։ Յայնժամ այպանեաց զնա Ատոմ՝ ասելով. Միթէ և այդ քարի՞նք իցեն, զի ես յառաջեցից։ Եւ արդ՝ եթէ դու զՄոկացիս կոչես դիւազգիս, ես զՍասանեանսդ կոչեմ կնամարդիս։ Եւ մտրակեալ զերիվարն՝ իբրև ընդ հովիտս ծաղկանց անցանէր զհուրն, զերծուցանելով զՇապուհ։

ԽՈՐԵՆԱՑԻ։

Ասի թէ Դիոգինէս յաւուրս ձմերայնոյ յերեկորեայ 'ի կարաս իջանէր վասն ցրտոյն, և 'ի տունջեան արտաքս ելանէր վասն արևուն։ Վասն որոյ և երբեմն ջեռնլով սորա, հասեալ Աղեքսանդրոս Մակեդոնացի՝

ստուեր առնէր 'ի վերայ նորա, զի մի՛ ջեռուցի՝ ասելով նմա. Ասա՛ Դիոգենէս, զի՞նչ կամիս, զի շնորհեցից քեզ: Եւ նա ասէ. Զայս ինչ շնորհեա՛ ինձ. փոքր ինչ 'ի բաց կացցես յինէն, զի ջեռայց: ՆՈՆՆՈՍ:

Կարկինոս՝ որ Թարգմանի Խեցգետին, ցանկայ ուտել զմիս զեռնոյ միոյ՝ որ անուանեալ կոչի Ոստրէոս. և քանզի դժուարորս է Ոստրէոսն, զի իբրև խեցեղէն պատեանս ունի շուրջ զիւրեաւ, և իբրև ընդ ամրածածուկ պարսպով զգուշացեալ պահի փափուկ մարմին իւրոյ կակուղ բնութեամբն, և մորթն 'ի վերայ սեպ և ողորկ խեցանման է, և այսպիսի իմն կոչէին զեռունն զայն Խեցեմորթ. և քանզի կերպարանս պատենից Գաղտակրի ունի՝ 'ի միջնորդունսն. զի այնպէս կազմեալ է զեռունն զայն Արարիչն: Եւ ոտք Խեցգետնոյն ոչ կարեն զամս գտանել յաղորկ և 'ի սեպ պատեան զեռնոյն, ժամապահ դարանակալ լինի, միտ դնէ՝ եթէ երբ ելցէ Ոստրէոսն 'ի խորոցն երթալ ցեզրն, որ անքոյթ իցէ 'ի հողմոյ: Եւ իբրև երթայ հասանէ յանքոյթ տեղին, սկսանի բանալ զպատեանսն՝ զոր ունի 'ի մկանունսն 'ի նմանութիւն Գաղտակրի՝ ընդդէմ արևուն, զի ջեռուցի: Յայնժամ երթայ վաղվաղակի Խեցգետինն, ընկենու քար ընդ անջրպետսն պատենիցն, զի մի՛ կարասցէ անդրէն զիւրեաւ ամփոփել զպատեանսն. և լինիցի նմա դիւրաւ ըմբռնել զՈստրէոսն, և ուտել:

ՄԵԾՆ ԲԱՐՍԵՂ:

Արարիչն Աստուած զերգական արարածոց կենդանեացս ազգ յերիս սեռս զանազանեալ որոշեաց. նախ՝ եղելոց հողեղինացն զօրութեանց զվերին կայանսն առ ինքեամբ և հուպ ընդ իւր տալով տեղի բնակութեան. Իսկ զգալեաց և անասուն կենդանեաց որ յերկրէ, սահմանեաց 'ի սոյնս՝ յորմէ ստեղծան, բազմանալ, և 'ի ծոց անդ մօրն դարձեալ լուծանել: Այլ զբանաւոր զայս մարդ յետոյ քան զնաւսն 'ի ներքս մուծեալ՝ որպէս ուսաք 'ի պատմութենէն, շաղկապումն և խառնուած արար սովաւ իմանալեաց և զգալեացն էութեանց: Վասնզի առ հող յերկրէ՝ ուստի անասնոց ջոկք գոյացան, և փչեաց յերեսս նորա շունչ կենդանի՝ որով իմանալի պատկերն Աստուծոյ 'ի նա էացաւ. և եղև մարդն հողեղէն՝ որպէս զանասունսն, և պատկերակից Աստուծոյ՝ որպէս զհրեշտակս, իմանալին այն հոգւով:

ԼԱՄԲՐՈՆԱՑԻ:

Զարմանալի և գեղեցիկ էր տեսիլ նորա. զի ունէր մարմին չափ հասակաւ, և մասունս անդամոցն պատշաճ: Ո՛չ կարի երկայն մարմնով՝ որ թուի անհեթեթ տեսանողացն, և ոչ փոքր՝ որ է արհամարհելի. այլ չափով ընտրութեան որոշեալ. և դիմացն պատկեր կարի զուարթ, և հեշտալի տեսողացն:

ԻԳՆԱՏԻՈՍ:

Ու երբ այս այսպէս պատրաստեցաւ, երկոքեան կողմանքն լի սրտմտութեամբ և մեծաւ բարկութեամբ զայրանային, և զազանացեալ զօրութեամբ յիրեարս յարձակէին երկոքեան. և ամբոխ աղաղակին յերկոցունց կողմանց իբրև 'ի մէջ ամպոց շփոթելոց ճայթմունս գործէր. և հնչումն ձայնից զքարանձաւս լերանցն շարժէր: 'Ի բազմութենէ սաղաւարտից, և 'ի փայլուն պատենազէն վառելոցն իբրև նշոյլք ճառագայթից արեգական հատանէին: Նաև 'ի բազում սուսերացն շողալ, և 'ի ճօճել բազմախուռն նիզակացն իբրև յերկնուստ ահագին հրաձգութիւնք եռային: Քանզի ո՞ իսկ է բաւական ասել զմեծամեծ տագնապ ահաւոր ձայնիցն, որպէս կոփիւնք վահանաւորացն, և ճայթմունք լարից աղեղանցն զլսելիս ամենեցուն առհասարակ խլացուցանէին: —Անդ էր տեսանել շտապ մեծի տագնապին, և զաղէտս անբաւ տարակուսանացն երկոցունց կողմանցն՝ առ'ի յանդուգն յարձակմանէն, զմիմեանս բաղխելով: Քանզի թանձրամիտքն յիմարէին, և վատասիրտքն լքանէին. քաջքն խիզախէին, և նահատակքն գոչէին: Ու խումբ արարեալ ամենայն բազմութեանն՝ ընդգետն 'ի մէջ փակէին. և զանգիտեալ գունդըն Պարսից 'ի դժուարութենէ գետոյն՝ ընդտեղեաւն զեռալ սկսան: Իսկ գունդն Հայոց հասեալ անցանէին, ձի 'ի վերայ առեալ՝ յարձակէին մեծաւ զօրութեամբ: Աստկապէս բաղխեալք ընդ միմեանս՝ յերկոցունց կողմանց բազում վիրաւորք յերկիր անկեալ դիաթաւալ խաղային ։ — Յայնմ մեծի տագնապի 'ի վեր հայեցաւ քաջն Վարդան, և տեսանէր զընտիր ընտիր քաջ նահատակաց Պարսից զօրուն՝ զի զճախակողմն շարժեցին զՀայոց գնդին. մեծաւ ուժով յարձակէր 'ի տեղին, և զաջ թեւն Պարսից գնդին բեկեալ՝ արկանէր զգազանօքն. և շրջան առեալ կոտորէր մինչև 'ի նոյն տեղի ։ Եւ այնպէս շատ տագնապի 'ի վերայ հասուցանէր, մինչև գունդն Մատեան քակեալ բաժանեցան 'ի մեծամուր պատրաստութենէն. դեռ ևս քաջ քաջ 'ի փախուստ դառնային ։ — Ապա դէտակն 'ի վեր համբառնայր Մուշկան Նիւսալաւուրտն, քակեալ զամենս տեսանէր 'ի գնդէն Հայոց, և զինքն մնացեալ 'ի հովիտս լերանց ։ Վասն որոյ զաղաղակ բարձեալ՝ քաջալերէր՝ շուրջ զիւրեաւ զզօրս Արեաց՝ որք զտեղի առեալ կային ընդդէմ գնդին Վարդանայ ։ Եւ անդէն 'ի տեղւոջն երկոքին կողմանքն զպարտութիւն խոստովանէին. և առ յոյժ թանձր անկեալ դիականց իբրև զքարակոյտս դերբկաց երևէին ։ — Զայն իբրև ետես Մուշկան Նիւսալաւուրտն, մնայր գազանացն Արտաշրի՝ որ 'ի վերայ գազանացն նստէր 'ի բարձր դիտանոցին, և կայր իբրև յամուր քաղաքին. և 'ի ձայն մեծ գալարափողոցն զիւր գունդն ստիպէր, և յառաջամարտիկ զօրօքն գնա 'ի մէջ փակէր ։ — Իսկ կորովին Վարդան իւրովք քաջ նիզակակցօքն ոչ սակաւ նախճիրս 'ի տեղւոջն գործեաց. յոբուն տեղւոջ և ինքն արժանի եղև առնուլ զկատարեալ նահատակութիւնն :

ԵՂԻՇԷ :

Եւ խմբեցաւ պատերազմն 'ի դաշտին՝ որ կոչի Ձիրաւ, և մատեան ճակատ առ ճակատ : Եւ մանկունքն քաջ Նախարարացն Հայոց ինքնակամ նահատակեալք մտին 'ի մէջ ճակատուցն առաջնորդութեամբ Սպարապետին իւրեանց Սմբատայ Րալեանի՝ որդւոյ Բագարատայ, որ յազգէն Բագրատունեաց : Ելին և 'ի զօրացն Պարսից համարք նոցա, և խաղացին 'ի մէջ ճակատուցն, և ցիր ընդ ցիր լինէր : Եւ 'ի դառնալ մանկանցն Պարսից, ընդ հուպ դարձեալ մերոցն զհետ նոցա՝ օրինակ իմն որպէս փոթորիկ յանտառէ տերևաթափ, այնպէս երագ յերկվարացն առեալ նիզակօք՝ դի ցուրտ յերկիր ընկենուին . ոչ կարելով նոցա յիւրեանց ճակատն մտանել : Իսկ յորժամ Պարսիկքն զմերն շրջէին, նոքա 'ի վահանափակն Յունաց իբր յամուր քաղաք մտանէին առ ոչինչ վնասելոյ : Վասնզի այնպէս արար Գորգոնոս իշխան հետևակ զօրուն, իբրև պարսպաւ պատեաց վահանօք զճակատն Պապայ : Վասնզի զօրքն Յունաց վառեալ էին 'ի զէնս ոսկւոյ և արծաթոյ . և երիվարք նոցա նոյնպէս զարդու : Եւ էր տեսանել իբրև զպարիսպ ինչ . յորոց յոլովք 'ի ջղեայ և 'ի կաշեայ պահպանակաց զգեստուն զկարծրութեան վիմաց բերէին երևոյթս . և 'ի վերայ նոցա անխալամ դէսք նշանք արձակեալք իբր զաղարթ ինչ հովանաւոր ծառոց։ Բայց զվիշապացն մանուածս ահագին բերանաբացութեամբ ուռուցեալ 'ի փչմանէ օդոյն՝ ոչ ինչ ուրեք կարեմ նմանեցուցանել, այլ միայն իբրեւ զլեառն ինչ անդամանդեայ խոնարհիլ 'ի ծով զբովանդակ ճակատն Յունաց 'ի Պարսկական զօրսն։ Քանզի եւ զնոսա էր տեսանել իբրեւ զհզօր ինչ գետ առ 'ի կողմն 'ի լայն ծաւալեալ. արդարեւ զջրոյ գոյն զրահաւորացն բերէր տեսութիւն։ — Արդ՝ իբրեւ ետես մեծն Ներսէս զայն ամենայն, ել նա 'ի կատար լերինն Նպատայ, եւ ամբարձ զձեռս իւր յերկինս՝ անխոնարհելի պահելով 'ի խնդրուածս հանգոյն նախամարգարէին Մովսիսի, մինչեւ պարտեցաւ երկրորդն Ամաղէկ։ — Իսկ 'ի ծագել արեգականն ընդդէմ մերոց զօրացն՝ 'ի պղնձապատ վահանացն նշոյլք զլերամբքն փայլատակէին իբրեւ յամպոյ մեծէ. եւ 'ի նոցանէ 'ի դուրս ոստէին 'ի մերոց Նախարարացն քաջ զրահաւորք՝ որպէս փայլատականց ճառագայթք։ Յորոց միայն 'ի տեսութենէն զանգիտեալ Պարսկական գունդն, սակաւ ինչ եւ մերն վասն ո՛չ կարել հայել ընդդէմ արեգական ծագմանն։ Իսկ 'ի բախելն զմիմեանս՝ եղեւ 'ի վերայ հովանի ամպոյ, եւ հողմ սաստիկ 'ի մերոցն կուսէ ընդդէմ Պարսկականին փչեալ։ Նա 'ի խառնակել մարտին՝ պատահէ Կամսարականն Սպանդարատ խմբի մեծի, յորում էր քաջ Տէրգիր Գ եկաց առջայ, զգլուխ միջի գնդին պնդութեամբ զտեղի ճակատուն կալեալ։ Նա յարձակեալ Սպանդարատ , և հերձեալ զխումբն՝ որպէս շանթահար յերկիր կործանէր զքաջն . և ընդխումբն պատուեալ՝ 'ի փախուստ դարձուցանէր : Եւ այսպէս 'ի վերին օգնականութենէն զօրացեալ հասարակ զօրքն Յունաց և Հայոց՝ դիակամբք թշնամեաց լցին զդաշտն ամենայն , և զմնացորդսն ամենայն 'ի փախուստ շրջեալ հալածեցին :

ԽՈՐԵՆԱՑԻ :

Շնորհեաց նմա պատկեր լուսազարդ , և հասակ փառաց անհամեմատ 'ի մէջ ամենայն մնեղեաց բանական ազգի . հարթ և ուղիղ հասակաւ , վայելուչ և պայծառ երեսօք . հեր գլխոյ նորա թխակերպ՝ գանգուրագեղ գիսաւորութեամբ աղեբեկ ջոկացեալ 'ի վերայ սպիտակափառ ճակատուն յոյժ խունախիտ թանձրութեամբ . մրազարդ կամարաձև կցուածք յօնիցն , և բիբք և արտեւանունք հանդերձ պողովք վկայեալք , երբև զշուշան 'ի հովիտս ծաղկեալ՝ ծաւալին հրաշազարդ յօրինմամբ . ունչք երկայնագոյնք և վայելչաւորք . լսելիք դիւրալուրք , և դիւրահաւանք 'ի բարիս , և պայծառք լուսահրաշ նմանեալ գունով . շրթունք նորա իբրև զլար կարմիր . ատամունք նորա հուպ առ միմեանս՝ զտեալք յաղտոյ . տեգք մուրուաց նորա զօրէն մանուշակի ծաղկեալք 'ի վերայ գունագեղ այտից՝ 'ի կերպս զուարթնոց տեսողացն զնա ցուցանէր :

ԱՐԾՐՈՒՆԻ :

Խայթեն բարկացողք իբրև զկարիճ, խածա-
նեն իբրև զօձս, հաչեն իբրև զշուն, պատա-
ռեն իբրև զգայլս, սրեն զատամունս իբրև
զվարազս, փրփրին իբրև զձիւահարս։ Ա-
րիւնուշտ աչքն, մաղձատեսակ դէմքն՝ զըր-
կեալ 'ի բնական գունոյն, անյօդ խօսքն՝ ա-
մենևին պակասեալ 'ի բանէ։ Դողան բոլոր
անդամքն, ոչ կարեն կալ յոտից վերայ, և
զմի տեղի ունել, այլ զօրէն արբեցող այսր
անդր դեգևին։ Ընդ վայր ածեն զձեռսն,
և 'ի հարուածս մերձաւորացն ձգեն։ Նա-
քան զձիւահարս ևս յանդգնաբար բերին,
և ատելիք տեսողացն երևին, որքան մինն
կամօք մոլեգնի, իսկ միւսն 'ի դիւէն լըբու-
թենէ։

ՍԱՐԳԻՍ։

Յորժամ տարերքըս դըղըրդին,
Հաստատութիւնքըն սասանին.
Երբ ըզծովու կոհակ կուտին
'Ի յեռանդանըն կաթսային.
Լայնատարած դողայ գետին,
'Ի թանձրութեանց հիմանց շարժին.
Մի ըզմիոյ հետ խափանին,
Կասեալ յերկուցըն տատանին.
Երկինք հիմամբքըդ զարհուրին,
Եւ ուժգնակի բախմամբ թընդին.
Կարծըր բնութիւնք վիմաց հալին,
Եւ ամենայն նիւթք հըրդեհին.
Մինչ գետք հրեղէնք յորդահոսին,
Երբ ըզհեղեղ ջուրց ծաւալին.
Հողմով հանդերձ սաստիկ հընչին,

Ու միգախառըն մըռմըռին .
Խըրթնահայեաց դիմօք վառին ,
Ուս թափանցիկ փայլաքերին .
Երբ ըղտերն մի բորբոքին
Բնութիւնք ամէն հողեղինին .
Բըլուրք լերամբքըն հալեսցին ,
Ու դաշտաձև աշխարհք լինին .
Ծովու ալիքըն ցամաքին ,
Ու կենդանիք նորա նուաղին :

ՇՆՈՐՀԱԼԻ :

Բայց թէ ըզդիրս իմ յանկաւոր
Ոք պատմեսցէ պատշաճաւոր ,
Կարծեմ թէ չէ՛ նըմանաւոր
Այս քաղաքաց որ երկրաւոր :
Լայն և արձակ նըստեալ յաթոռ ,
Որպէս 'ի կառըս թագաւոր .
Կամ թագուհի յոյժ գեղաւոր ,
Ոսկէտըռոռն և ճամկաւոր ,
Փողփողելով 'ի վերջաւոր ,
Պայծառազգեստ և պըճնաւոր :
Շուրջանակի պարառաւոր
Պարիսպ ածեալ լայն և ամուր :
Աշտարակօք բարձր ահաւոր ,
Իմաստապէս ւարուեստաւոր :
Որպէս ըզգըլուխըն գիսաւոր ,
Մակաւասար անձին բոլոր .
Հաստահեղոյս հիմամբ ւ'ի խոր ,
Մահարձանօք պըսակաւոր .
Տունք և տաճարք զարմանաւոր ,
Շինեալ 'ի գիրկս իմ շքեղաւոր :

ՆՈՅՆՆ :

Ցընծա՛ խորանըդ լուսոյ,
Բերկրեա՛ տաճարըդ արեւու.
Խընդա՛ աթոռդ Աստուծոյ,
Բարձող Բանին Բարձրելոյ...
Բուրվառ խընկոց անուշից,
Քառաբուրեանըն խառնից.
Օր ծերունեացըն խըմբից
Զաղօթս խընկեն քոյ բանից:

ՆՈՅՆՆ:

Եպիսկոպոսապետ Վրթանէս, եւ որք ընդ նմա Եպիսկոպոսունք, եւ ամենայն Նախարարք Հայոց՝ Տեառն մերոյ Կոստանդեայ Կայսեր Ինքնակալի խնդալ:

Յո՛ւշ լիցի քեզ պայման ուխտի հօրն քո Կոստանդիանոսի՝ որ առ մերում Թագաւորին Տրդատայ. եւ մի՛ տացես զաշխարհն քո Պարսից անաստուածից, այլ օգնեսցես մեզ զօրօք՝ թագաւորեցուցանել զորդի Տրդատայ զԽոսրով: Քանզի Աստուած զձեզ ո՛չ միայն Եւրոպիայ, այլեւ ամենայն Միջերկրեայց տիրեցոյց. եւ ահ զօրութեան ձերոյ եհաս մինչեւ 'ի ծագս երկրի: Եւ մեք խընդրեմք առաւել քան զառաւել տիրել ձեզ: Ո՛ղջ լերուք:

ԽՈՐԵՆԱՑԻ:

Օգոստոս Ինքնակալ Կայսր Կոստանդու Մեծի Վրթանիսի, եւ ամենայն համօրէն աշխարհականաց քոց խնդալ:

Առաքեցի ձեզ զօր յօգնականութիւն, եւ հրաման թագաւորեցուցանել ձեզ զԽոս.

րովու որդի արքային ձերոյ Տրդատայ, որպէս զի բարեկարգութիւն հաստատեալ՝ մեզ ծառայեսցէք միամտութեամբ ։ Ողջ լերուք ։

ՆՈՅՆՆ ։

Աստրատեղասն Գաղաւոն, և ամենայն Նախարարք Հայոց մասինն Յունաց՝ Տեառն մերում Խոսրովայ արքայի կողմանն Պարսից խնդալ ։

Տէր գիտէ զմտերմութիւն մեր առ յիշել թագաւորին մերում Արշակայ՝ զոր մինչև ցօր վախճանին անշիջելի պահեցաք. և արդ խորհեալ եմք նոյնպէս ծառայել քեզ միամտութեամբ, եթէ հաստատեսցես առ մեզ դաշանցս զերկոս զայսոսիկ ։ Առաջին՝ չյիշել զյանցանս մեր, զոր պատերազմեցաք ընդ քեզ 'ի հարկէ, և ոչ 'ի կամաց ։ Երկրորդ՝ զի դարձուցես 'ի մեզ զամենայն ժառանգութիւնս մեր՝ որ 'ի մասինդ Պարսից, զոր հատեք յարքունիս ։ Երրորդ՝ հնարել թափել զմեզ 'ի Կայսերէ, զի մի վրդովեսցեն զբնակութիւնս՝ որք ունիմք իշխանութիւն յայսմ բաժնի ։ Եւ զայս պայման ուխտի գրել, և խաչ հաստատել՝ կնքեսցես. զորս տեսեալ՝ փութասցուք 'ի ծառայութ̅ի ձեր ։ Ողջ լեր Տէր մեր ։

ՆՈՅՆՆ ։

Քաջ արանց Խոսրով Հայոց արքայ Սուր
տեղատի Գաղաւոնի , և ամենայն Նախա
րարաց մերոց ողջոյն ։

Շատ ուրախ լերուք , զի և մեք ողջ եմք
և ուրախացաք ընդ լուր ողջունի ձերոյ ,
առաքեցաք ըստ խնդրոյ ձերոյ զայս պայմա
ուխտի ։ Առաջին՝ չյիշել զյանցանս ձեր
զոր չունէաք առ յանցանս իսկ , այլ երախ
տաւորս զմիամտելն առ Թագաւորին Արշ
կունւոյ՝ զոր պաշտէիքն . զի և առ մեզ զնոյ
յուսամք լինել ։ Երկրորդ՝ դարձուցանել
ձեզ զժառանգութիւնս ձեր , զոր ունիւ
յարքունիս՝ բաց յայնմանէ , զոր ումեք ու
մեք պարգևեցաք . և ոչ շրջին պարգևք Թ
գաւորաց առանց վնասու . մանաւանդ զի
դիւան հօրն մերոյ Տեառն Շապհոյ արքայ
արքայի եմուտ . այլ փոխանակ ընդ այնր
յարքունուստ լնումք և զձերոյն պակասու
թիւնն ։ Երրորդ՝ թափեմք զձեզ 'ի գործ
կալացն Յունաց՝ թէպէտ պատերազմաւ ըն
Կայսեր , թէպէտ խաղաղութեամբ ։ — Ն
զքեզ՝ Գաղաւոն , արիւն իմ և հարազա
տութիւն՝ ոչ ըստ վաղնջուց ազգականու
թեանն , այլ ըստ արդեանս՝ որ 'ի մօրէ քու
մէ Արշանուշայ Արշակունւոյ , հանեալ ըն
քեզ 'ի հայրենեաց քոց Կամսարականաց ,
'ի մայրենիս քո յիմս առեալ ազգ՝ Արշա
կունի անուամբ պատուեցից ։

ՆՈՅՆՆ ։

Ընուլ զայս իմաստ աստուածային քո ըն-
ձից պա՛րտ համարեցայ՝ ով Գրիգորիոս, քա-
հանայապետական գլուխ և սիւն հաստա-
տութեան Եկեղեցւոյ ։ Սակայն ունիմք առ-
այս և զհակառակորդայն զբանն՝ որք ոչ
սակաւ տան ամբոխումն խորհրդոցն, որ 'ի
մեզն շարժմանն ։ Քանզի է նոցա առ ամե-
նայն բան զներհակն մերձ դնել · եթէ եր-
կայնագունից հանդխոլին բանից, զամէն փա-
քու համանել և անցանել · իսկ եթէ սուղ
լիցի բանն, իբրու ոչ պարունակող զիմաստս,
և ոչ բաւականացեալ առ լցոյն՝ պարսա-
ւեալ լինի ։ Դարձեալ առ այս՝ եթէ նորա-
գոյնս ինչ ունիցի, զկարգն առաջի դնեն՝ իբ-
րև զխրթահասս, վասն այնորիկ և օգտա-
կարս · ապա եթէ պարզագոյն լիցի, զամէնն
է նոցա իմաստասիրական եղանակ բանից՝ իբ-
րև զօրաւորս և արուեստականս ։ Արդ՝ այս-
չափ է նոցա զատելն, ոչ վասն առաջիկայ ի-
րիս, այլ միայն՝ զի ընտրողս և ճանաչողս ցու-
ցեալ լինիցին ։ Իսկ մեզ զի լիցի զանձինս ան-
ըմբռնելի ունել 'ի նոցա կարծեայն, որչափ
ինչ ունիմք ուղղել՝ զմիջինն այսոցիկ տեսու-
թեանց ընտրեսցուք զբանն · ոչ յոյժ ամփո-
փել, և ոչ կարի երկայնել · դարձեալ՝ մի 'ի
ծածկելն փութալ, սակայն 'ի գեղջկայն
հեռագոյնս դնել նուաստ բանից ։ Այսու յա-
ղագս այսոցիկ այսչափ ։

ԻԳՆԱՏԻՈՍ ։

Քանզի բազում ինչ գործք յաւուրս Ար-
տաշխսի գործեցան, վասն այնորիկ 'ի բա-

զում ճառս կոտորեցաք՝ զի մի երկայնութ
բանից տաղտկութիւն ընթերցողացն լինի
ցի · որոյ է վերջին ճառս այսպիսի ինչ՝ յի
շատակել և զայլսն ևս որ ինչ 'ի ժամանակ
Արտաշիսի ։ Զի թէպէտ և զայլն ամենայն
զոր ինչ յիշատակեցաք յառաջագոյն ճա
ռիցն , կարգք և սովորութիւնք գեղեցիկ
հաստատեցան 'ի Վաղարշակայ , և յայլո
առաջնոց թագաւորացն , այլ 'ի մեծամե
արուեստից և 'ի գիտութեանց ունայնա
ցեալք էին , որպէս հինից և ասպատակա
պարապեալք · և այսպիսի գիտութեանց կամ
անփոյթ արարեալք , և կամ ո՛չ հասեալք
զՇաբաթուց ասեմ և զԱմսոց և զՏարեա
բոլորմանց ։ Քանզի ո՛չ այսպիսի ինչ ճանա
չէր առ նոսա՝ այլոց ազգաց վարելով · և ո՛չ
'ի ծովակս աշխարհիս նաւագնացութիւնք
և ո՛չ 'ի վերայ գետոց ճանապարհորդութիւնք
և ո՛չ գործիք ձկանց որսոց · այլև ո՛չ յամե
նայն տեղիս երկրագործութիւնք , բայց դոյզ
ուրեք , ըստ օրինակի հիւսիսականաց կող
մանց շաղղակերութեամբ և այլովք այսպի
սեօք կեցեալք ։ Եւ այս ամենայն յօրինե
յաւուրս Արտաշիսի ։

ԽՈՐԵՆԱՑԻ ։

Եւ մինչդեռ 'ի խրձիթէ անտի արտաք
հանեալ՝ չուեալ ածէին (զՄողոմոն ճգնա
ւոր) յաթոռ Հայրապետութեան , հարցա
յոմանց աշատաց՝ թէ վասն զի ծեր ես , և
յանհնարին ճգնողական վարուց յոյժ անա
ւագեալ , ընդէ՞ր յօժարեալ երթաս 'ի Հայ

բարետութիւն : Եւ որ պատասխանեաց նորա ասէր . Երթամ, զի գեղապաճոյճ նկարողաց սեւել զիս ընդ այլ հայրապետսն տամ յորմ եկեղեցւոյն : Եւ ըստ նմին այսմ գործն կատարէր . զի ոչ աւելի քան զմի ամ կեցեալ՝ փոխի յաշխարհէս , և գնի ընդ հարս իւր , և կենդանագրի ՚ի քուարանի սրբում :

ՅՈՎՀԱՆՆԷՍ ԿԱԹՈՂԻԿՈՍ :

Փիլիպպոս և Ողոմպիաս Արիստոտէլի վարդապետի խնդալ :

[illegible]՝ որ ՚ի վերայ կացուցաք խնամածու պատանւոյդ , զմեր՝ զոր ինչ տամք ընդէմ սա ձեզ , այդպես ոչ բաւական լինել Աղեքսանդրի՝ վասն բողոքում պարգևս կամեցեալ տալ : Արդ՝ հասեալ յայդը վերայ , բարեաց կարգեա , և նշանակեա մեզ :

ՎԱՐԴ. ԱՂԵՔՍԱՆԴՐԻ :

Վարդապետ Արիստոտէլէս Փիլիպպոսի և Ողոմպիայ խնդալ :

Ո՛չ կարծեմ՝ յիմոց ձեռաց խրատ առնել որդւոյ ձերոյ Աղեքսանդրի՝ օտար ինքեան , և իմոյս , և ձերոյ բարուցդ արտաքոյ ինչ գործեալ . քանզի լսեմ , և զուսմունս սորա տեսանելով՝ դատող քննութեամբ առնել , և ոչ իբրև զմանուկ . այլ իբրև զհին այր ընտրել և դատել կարէ : Արդ՝ զոր ինչ և ձեզ հաճոյ թուեսցի , զայն գործեսջիք : Ողջ լերուք :

ԱՆԴ :

Փիլիպպոս և Ոլոմպիաս Զևքսեսի մերոյ խնդալ։

Առաքեցաք Արիստոտելի վարդապետի գրեալ թուղթն 'ի քէն առ մեզ, որպէս զի զայս ընկալեալ՝ գրեալսն 'ի նմա ջանասցի յուղղութիւն ածել։ Ողջ լեր։

Արիստոտելէս Աղեքսանդրի որդւոյ խնդալ։

Գրեցին առ իս ծնողքն քո, զի զառաքեալ թոշակն 'ի նոցանէ քեզ ոչ լինել բաւական. զոր ոչ կարծեմ արտաքոյ՝ ոչ քոյոց և ոչ իմոց, և ոչ ծնողացն քոց կամաց այլազգ ինչ առնել։ Ողջ լեր ինձ որդի՛ քաղցրենի։

Աղեքսանդրոս մեծահանճար վարդապետիդ իմոյ խնդալ։

Գիտեմ հա՛յր՝ անարժան գոլ զառաքեալ թոշակն իմ 'ի ծնողացն իմոց. և սակայն զայս լուեալ՝ պարտ և արժան էր բարկանալ, եթէ յաղագս իւրեանց որդւոյ։ Բայց արդ զընդդէմն գրեցին։ Ողջ լինել քեզ աղաչեմ։

Փիլիպպոս և Ոլոմպիա Աղեքսանդրի որդւոյ խնդալ։

Զկարգեալսն քեզ թոշակ՝ զորս 'ի մէնջ առաքեմք, արժանիս Փիլիպպոսի և Ոլոմպիադայ վարկեալ՝ մի՛ արտամերժեալ 'ի բաց առաքեր, և մի՛ զԱրիստոտելեայ թուղթս. այլ որպէս քեզ վայել է, պահեա՛. և զայլսն

Եւ ինչ լաւս ընդ միտ ածեալ՝ խորհեցայ։
Ո՛ղջ լեր մեզ քաղցր և իմաստուն որդեակ։

ԱՆԴ։

Աղեքսանդրոս Փիլիպպոսի և Ողոմպիադայ ծնողաց։

Ո՜ կարգեալ Թուղթս՝ զոր տայք ինձ 'ի ձեռն Ո՜ կքսեայ, ոչ արժանի Աղեքսանդրի, և որպէս՝ վայելէ՝ զայս մատակարարել Փիլիպպոսի և Ողոմպիադայ։ Այլ զԱրիստոտելի զվարդապետեսն իմոյ զպատուիրանս ընդ միտ ածեմ, և խորհիմ արժանի ուսմանն ընձեռողին, և զձեզ պախարակեմ, որ գիրաւ զանելով 'ի վայր տայք այլոց երբեմն վատաբարոյից և շողոմողաց. և զայլս յաղագս որդւոյ՝ որ ըստ բնութենէ պարտիք, լաւ լինել՝ յաղագս նախախնամութիւն և հոգ մատուցանել, որ ինձ օգուտ բերէ։ Ողջ լինել ձեզ ըղձիւք խնդրեմ։

ԱՆԴ։

Աչքըն ծով 'ի ծով ծիծաղախիտ
Ուաւալմայր յուսաւորուն,
Երկու փայլակնաձև արեգական նման ...
Բերանն երկթերթի, վարդն 'ի շրթանց կաթէր,
Լեզուին շարժողին քաղցրերգանայր տաւիղն։
Ծոցըն լուսափայլ, կարմիր վարդով լցեալ,
Ողկքըն ծիրանի մանուշակի հոյլք։

ՆԱՐԵԿԱՑԻ։

Ածցուք զթանգարական վաճառս համ-
թից, վաճառեսցուք լսելեաց զգիտս աշ-
խատութեան մերոյ՝ առնուլ զունկնդրու-
թիւն, և տալ զպատմութիւն, մանաւանդ
վասն քոյոյ հրամանիդ՝ քա՛ջ արանց Տրդատ
արքայ Հայոց Մեծաց։ Առեալ զշահ վա-
ճառին աշխարհի շինութեան՝ քեզ 'ի գան-
յաւելցուք 'ի մերոց ծովավաստակ նաւաս-
տեացս։

ԱԳԱԹԱՆԳԵՂՈՍ։

Իբրև չոգան տարան յերկիրն Պարսից զա-
մենայն գերութիւնն Հայոց, և զՕուխթ
երէց Արտաշատ քաղաքի ունէին կապանօք
առաջի թագաւորին Պարսից Շապհոյ։ Եւ
նայէր թագաւորն Շապուհ, և տեսանէր
զերէցն Օուխթ այր բարձր և անձնեայ, և
'ի տիոց մանուկ. և հերք գլխոյն ալևորեալ
էին, այլ մօրուքն դեռ տակաւին սեաւ և
կային։ Ապա յորժամ զառաջինն խօսել
սկսաւ, ասէ՝ թէ տեսանէ՞ք զառնդ զայդ-
զչարութիւնն. քանզի այտի 'ի հերացն երևի
թէ կախարդ է. զի հերքն սպիտակ են, և
մօրուքն սեաւ։ Իսկ երէցն տուեալ պատաս-
խանի՝ ասէ, թէ քեզ պէ՞տ իցէ, այլ զի՞նչ
կամիս խօսել և առնել, խօսեա՛ց։ Այլ վասն
այդորիկ դիտեա՛, զի յիրաւունս սպիտակա-
ցեալ են նախ հերքս, զի բազում աւուրբք
երէց են՝ զո՞նեայ հնգետասան ամօք, քան
զմօրուսս նախաբոյս են։

ԲՈՒԶԱՆԴ։

Նորահրաշ պսակաւոր և զօրագլուխ առա-
քինեաց ,
Մատեցար զինու հոգւոյն արիաբար ընդ-
դէմ մահու .
Մարտեան քաջ նահատակ որ վանեցեր ըզ-
թշնամին ,
Մարգագոյն արեամբըդ քով պսակեցեր
զԵկեղեցին :
Երկնաւոր թագաւորին զինու յաղթեալ
պատերազմին ,
Խոհական իմաստութեամբ խոհեմացեալ
անճառապէս .
Խորին խորհրդական և ծանուցեալ ա-
նուն բարի ,
Խաչելոյն վիճակ եղեալ հեղմամբ արեան
պսակեցաւ :
Բնական լուսով լցեալ արիացեալըն քաջն
Բաբակ ,
Թաթաւեալ ՚ի կարմրութիւն բոսորային
բղխեալ աղբիւրն .
Զփրկականն ըմպեալ զբաժակ և մը-
կրտեալ արեամբն իւրով ,
Դասակցեալ ընդ անմարմնոցն Երրոր-
դութեանն երգել ըզփառս :
Սրբափայլ զգեստուք պճնեալ՚ի յերկ-
նաւոր հանդիսադրին ,
Երրորդութեամբըն զօրացեալ, վանեալ
զամուրըս Բանսարկուին .
Հրմայեակ հօր ընծայեալ Աստուծոյ դո-
լով չարչարակից ,
Հոգւով յաղթեալ պատերազմին և չա-
րասէր թագաւորին :

Լական բարւոյն դիտմամբ ընդդէմ մեղա-ցըն վառեցաւ ,
Տարագնաց ելիւք յերկինըս պարակցեալ ընդ անմարմնոցն .
Տաճատ զարմանալի տաճար եղեալ Երրորդութեանն ,
Տէրունեան սուրբ խորհրդոյն տուն և տեղի արժանացեալ ։
Ստացեալ ըզհաւատոյ վահան յուսոյն զրա-հիւք ծածկեալ ,
Զփրկականըն սաղաւարտ 'ի գլուխ ե-դեալ զնըշան խաչին .
Վահան վեհ երևեալ, նոր մանկութեամբ նահատակեալ,
Խաչելոյն վըկայ եղեալ պըսակեցաւ ա-րեամբն իւրով ։
'Ի հոտ անոյշ ողջակիզեալ մատուցանէր զինքըն նըւէր ,
Բանաւոր պատարագաւ ընծայելով Հօր 'ի յերկինըս .
Արսէնըն ցանկալի արդարութեամբըն ճո-խացեալ ,
Իմաստութեամբ պայծառացեալ յեւթ-նարփեան շնորհաց Հոգւոյն ։
Երկոքումբք հարազատօք ընտրելագոյն նա-հատակօք ,
Յառաջեալ յամենեցունց գլուխ և ա-ւարտ Մարտիրոսաց .
Նախաշաւիղ գոլով բարեաց յառաջա-դէմըն Գարեգին ,
Ընկալեալ ըզվըրաբիմըն յաղթանակ նա-հատակաց ։

Բամկական խումբ հաղորդաց և երեմնից Թիւ-
ընդ. վեցից ,
Որք ընդ Նոսին նահատակեալք արիաբար
պատերազմաւ.
Եւ հեղլին զարիւնս իւրեանց 'ի Նորոգումն
Եկեղեցւոյ ,
Ընդ Նոսին պսակելով 'ի յերկնաւոր հան-
դիսադրէն ։

Գոհութեամբ փառաւորութիւն Երրորդու-
թեանդ նըւագեմք ,
Բազմութեամբ պսակելոցս ընդ մեզ մա-
ծեալ տաւղինեայ .
Եկեղեցիք Հայաստանեայց պայծառա-
պէս զարդարեցան ,
Ննջելով մինչ բարեխօս ընձեռնութիւն
մեղաց սոցա ։

ՇԱՐԱԿԱՆ ։

INDEX